ASSAULT ON RURAL POVERTY

The Case of Ethiopia

Haileleul Getahun

University Press of America,® Inc.
Lanham · New York · Oxford

Copyright © 2001 by
University Press of America,® Inc.
4720 Boston Way
Lanham, Maryland 20706

12 Hid's Copse Rd.
Cumnor Hill, Oxford OX2 9JJ

Library of Congress Cataloging-in-Publication Data

Hailemariam Getahun.
Assault on rural poverty : the case of Ethiopia / Haileleul Getahun.
p.   cm
Includes index.
l. Poverty—Ethiopia. 2. Rural poor—Ethiopia. 3. Ethiopia—Rural
conditions. 4. Land reform—Ethiopia. 5. Ethiopia—Economic
policy. I. Title.
HC845.Z9 P624   2001   338.1'863—dc21   2001027035 CIP

ISBN 0-7618-1980-0 (cloth: alk. paper)

Contents

Illustrations

List of Tables and Figures

Tables

List of Abbreviations

AAPO	All Amhara Peoples Organization
ACC	Administrative Coordinating Committee
AFDB	African Development Bank
ADLI	Agricultural Development Led-Industry
AEFA	All Ethiopian Farmer Association
AIDB	Agricultural and Industrial Development Bank
AMC	Agricultural Marketing Corporation
BHN	Basic Human Needs
CADU	Chilalo Agricultural Development Unit
CEAL	Economic Community of Central African States
COEDF	Coalition of Ethiopian Democratic Forces
COR	Council of Representatives
DBE	Development Bank of Ethiopia
DSC	Development Support Communication
DTCP	Development Training and Communication Planning
ECA	Economic Commission for Africa of the United Nations

EEC	European Economic Community
ECOWAS	Economic Community of West African States
EDU	Ethiopian Democratic Union
ENATAD	Ethiopian National Alliance to Advance Democracy
EPID	Extension and Project Implementation Department
EPLF	Eritrean Peoples Liberation Front
EPRDF	Ethiopian Peoples Revolutionary Democratic Front
EPRP	Ethiopian Peoples Revolutionary Party
FAO	Food and Agriculture Organization of the United Nations
FA	Farmers Association
GDP	Gross Domestic Product
GNP	Gross National Product
HDI	Human Development Index
IBRD	International Bank for Reconstruction and Development (World Bank)
IFAD	International Fund for Agricultural Development
IMF	International Monetary Fund
JUNIC	Joint United Nations Information and Communication
LADB	Lesotho Agricultural Development Bank
LPA	Lagos Plan of Action
MEDHIN	Ethiopian Median Democratic Party
MEISON	All Ethiopian Socialist Movement
NBK	National Bank of Kenya
NGO	Non-Government Organization
OAU	Organization of African Unity
OECD	Organization for Economic Cooperation and Development
OLF	Oromo Liberation Front
PA	Peasant Association
PDRE	People's Democratic Republic of Ethiopia

PMAC	Provisional Military Administrative Council
PTA-ESA	Preferential Trade Area for Eastern and Southern Africa
RRC	Relief and Rehabilitation Commission
SAP	Structural Adjustment Program
SEPDF	Southern Ethiopia Peoples Democratic Coalition
SIDA	Swedish International Development Agency
SUAM	States Union of the Arab Maghbreb
TGE	Transitional Government of Ethiopia
TPLF	Tigrean (or Tigrayan) Peoples Liberation Front
USAID	United States Agency for International Development
UN	United Nations
UNDP	United Nations Development Program
UNESCO	United Nations Education, Scientific and Cultural Organization
UNFPA	United Nations Fund for Population Activities
UNICEF	United Nations Childrens Fund
USSR	United Soviet Socialist Republic
WACRRD	World Conference on Agrarian Reform and Rural Development
WFP	World Food Program
WHO	World Health Organization of the United Nations
WPE	Workers Party of Ethiopia

Preface

This book outlines and analyzes the various causes of rural poverty and constraints impeding agricultural productivity during the last four decades under three different regimes. It first examines the feudalistic system under Emperor Haile Selassie; then the command economic system of the military junta led by Mengistu Hailemariam; and finally the current capitalistic system of the Federal Republic of Ethiopia led by Meles Zenawi. It discusses the lessons drawn from Ethiopian experience during these three regimes, as well as from other African and Asian countries. These provide the basis for recommending a *small farmer-led agricultural and rural development strategy* that, if implemented, would alleviate rural poverty in Ethiopia. The author maintains that the keys for successful development are the *provision of institutional savings and credit* for small-scale farmers and small business owners; the *deep involvement of the community* in project planning, implementation, evaluation and sharing of the benefits; and the use of *development support communication* for motivation, information dissemination, and training. The author argues strongly that ethnic politics in Ethiopia is destructive of Ethiopian society and militates against sustainable development. Rather, the path to peace and sustainable development requires that ethnic politics be scrapped and replaced by a genuinely democratic and widely acceptable system of governance.

Acknowledgments

A great number of individuals and organizations assisted me while I was undertaking this study in the United States, for which I am very grateful. Although the views expressed in this book are my own, I would like to especially acknowledge here the contributions of a few individuals.

I would like to extend my deep appreciation to Professor James Quirin of Fisk University for his timely assistance and encouragement. His generous advice was critical to the success of my work. I was allowed access to his resources and library that contributed a great deal to my research.

The manuscript has benefited immeasurably from comments and criticism provided by John Bruce from the Land Tenure Center, at the University of Wisconsin-Madison.

I owe special thanks to Alemante Gebre Selassie of William and Mary College for his valuable comments on the land tenure sections of the manuscript. I have greatly benefited from the comments and suggestions of Aklog Birara of the World Bank for which I thank him.

I am particularly grateful to Lane E. Holdcroft, an inspiring and longtime friend and retired senior USAID officer, whom I worked with when he was posted in Ethiopia. He has spent much of his time since the inception of this study editing and improving all of the draft chapters, and then preparing the manuscript for publication. Without his assistance and guidance, this study would have not been completed. For that I owe him a very special thanks.

Last, but not least, my thanks go to my dear wife, Aster Teklemariam, and our children, Nardos, Sebuh, Eyeluta, and Hosanna Haileleul for their enduring love and support during the writing of the book.

Hermitage, Tennessee
November 2000

Maps of Ethiopia

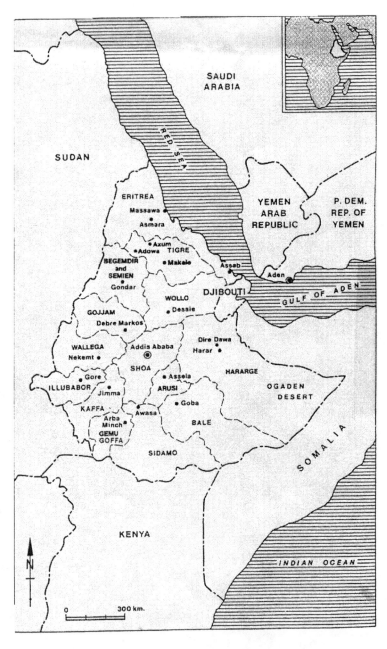

Map 1. Administrative Divisions of Ethiopia, 1974

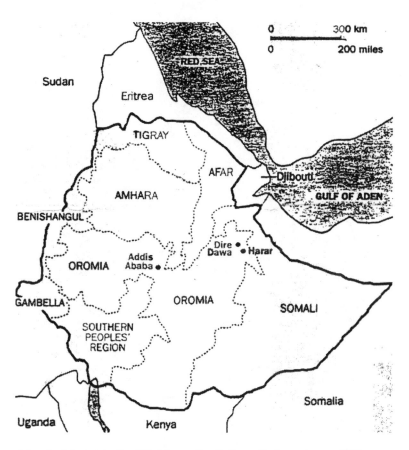

Map 2. Administrative Divisions after Eritrean Independence, 1993

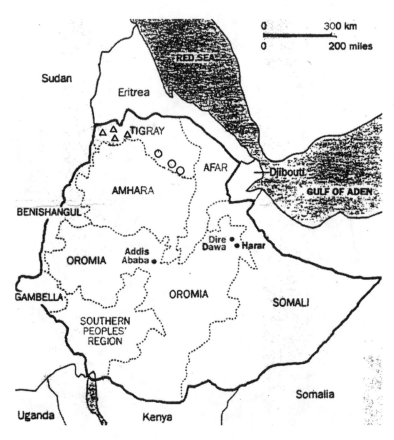

Map 3. Administrative Divisions Showing Annexed Districts, 1997

Chapter 1

Introduction

1.1 A Nation in Crisis

It is commonplace to hear that Ethiopia is in crisis. Yet the food crisis in that nation has been around for centuries. Hunger and malnutrition have always been a feature of Ethiopian history. During the 1970s and 1980s, and to a lesser degree in the 1990s, we have witnessed terrifying famines brought about by what 1998 Nobel Laureate economist Amartya Sen refers to as "food availability declines".[1] In Ethiopia "food availability declines" have many causes. The most obvious of these are drought; political instability; wrong-headed economic and social policies; weak production technology development and transfer systems; poor credit and marketing services; inadequate physical infrastructure; lack of human and institutional capacity; plus unproductive land tenure systems and land fragmentation.[2] The world will never forget the horrifying scenes of famines shown on television screens around the world in 1973-74, 1984-85, and 1987-1990 that claimed the lives of some two million Ethiopians. Recurrent drought and famine in Ethiopia lessened during the 1990s. However, again in the summer of the year 2000, an estimated eleven million Ethiopians were at risk of starvation in southeastern Ethiopia.[3]

Over the past 40 years, Ethiopia has remained one of the world's most underdeveloped countries with widespread poverty, hunger and malnutrition. In 1980, it had the sixth lowest per capita income of any country in the world. Then in 1983, it gained the dubious distinction of having the world's lowest per capita income, US$120. In 1997, among African nations, only Mozambique had a lower per capita income than Ethiopia's US$110 – compared to US$500 for all of sub-Saharan Africa.[4]

Historically, even under normal conditions when natural calamities such as drought and famine were not a major problem, often Ethiopia has been unable to feed its population. Yet Ethiopia is a nation of vigorous, resilient people with considerable natural resources, and thus it has great potential. The country's agriculture could support a much larger population if the causes of low productivity noted above were adequately addressed. If appropriate policies and programs to address these causes were successfully implemented, Ethiopia could produce sufficient food for its growing population and even a surplus for export on a sustainable basis.

Ethiopia today remains a predominately agrarian subsistence economy. About 84 percent of the population is rural. Agriculture continues to dominate the economy. In 1997, agriculture accounted for 56 percent of gross domestic product, compared to about 50 percent in 1975.[5] Peasant farms are of overwhelming importance in Ethiopia's agricultural sector.[6] They account for around 95 percent of the cultivated area. During the 1970s, the military government introduced two new types of production units, producer cooperatives and state farms. By 1990, producer cooperatives and state farms accounted for about five percent of cultivated area.[7]

During the reign of Emperor Haile Selassie, 1930-1974, absentee landlordism in the south and southwest was the major obstacle to agricultural progress. The majority of the rural population lived as sharecroppers with income barely sufficient to provide for a narrowly defined subsistence minimum. The peasants paid rent in cash, or in-kind as a share of the crop. Tenant farmers had little incentive to invest in increasing productivity and technological innovations when a large proportion of every increase in production automatically went to the landowner. An additional disincentive was that the tenants had little or no security of tenure.[8]

Following the military junta's land reform of 1975, the importance of both producer cooperatives and state farms grew while the peasant sector declined.[9] After adoption of socialism as its guiding ideology, the military junta's policy was to concentrate its resources on state farms and producer cooperatives. Its long-term objective was to transform the entire peasant sector into a cooperative sector.[10] This effort was patterned after the rigid Soviet-style economic system. There is widespread agreement that typically such schemes have been expensive, and have not achieved the expected production output, nor have they raised farmer income to targeted levels. Nonetheless, the 1975 land reform proclamation did bring about fundamental changes in the rural structure of Ethiopia by abolishing tenancy, hired labor, and landlords.

Unfortunately, the 1975 land reform also launched a new folly. Farmers were forced to combine their plots of land and live in communal villages. They were told what to grow and forced to sell to the government at a (low) fixed price. The policies of the *Derg* were intended to boost production through collective efforts. The reason for encouraging large-scale collective farms was based on the assumption that these farms would be superior to small-scale family farms. Yet it is widely acknowledged around the world that the family farm, whether or not supplemented by hired labor, has proven to be the most efficient form of organization for agricultural production – both in comparison with large-scale collectivized agriculture and with large-scale corporate land ownership.[11] Taiwan, South Korea, China, and Japan are typical examples of nations with highly productive small family farms.

The fundamental problem of agriculture in agrarian economies has always been that the subsistence peasant sector traditionally produced only a meager economic surplus. Therefore, in agrarian economies only by significant increases in the productivity of smallholder agriculture can any major increases in domestic production be achieved that would provide an economic surplus. By the 1970s, the importance of small farmer development and its potential contribution to poverty alleviation and economic growth was generally understood by development scholars and donor agency practitioners.[12]

Robert S. McNamara, then president of the World Bank, stated:

Without rapid progress in smallholder agriculture throughout the developing world, there is little hope either of achieving long-term economic growth or significantly reducing the level of absolute poverty. The fact is that very little has been done over the past two decades specifically designed to increase the productivity of subsistence agriculture.[13]

Nonetheless, even today major increases in smallholder productivity, in yields per unit of land or labor, remain largely unrealized in much of sub-Saharan Africa. This is because the strategic role of smallholder agriculture as "an engine of economic growth" has not been widely recognized by sub-Saharan African policy makers and national planners. For too long, sub-Saharan African government leaders have given too little attention to agriculture in general and their large smallholder sectors in particular. The widespread lack of support for developing small farmer agriculture by African political leaders has been a continuing concern of most donor agencies.[14]

The Ethiopian peasant farmer uses the same seeds, plows and farming methods as his forefathers have for centuries. Production technologies are simple; capital consists of rudimentary implements (a sickle, a wooden plow, and a machete); power is limited to that provided by an inadequate number of draft animals; seeds are broadcast by hand and almost no fertilizer is used. There are also problems the farmer can't solve alone, e.g., storage, transport and marketing. Rain in Ethiopia is unpredictable; some years it does not come at all, and in others it comes with such force that it takes half the topsoil with it, and serious crop pests abound.

In the last four decades, three successive governments in Ethiopia have failed to employ policies and implement programs that give adequate attention to development and dissemination of improved production technology for the small farmer, and other measures needed to increase small farmer food crop production. Both the imperial government and the military junta failed to help smallholders develop and apply "green revolution" technology. The current government's commitment to expand its agricultural technology dissemination program for small farmers is commendable, but it requires more resources and other supporting measures.

Increased crop yields come from a combination of inputs, i.e., fertilizer, improved seed varieties, irrigation, pest control, and better crop management. This is how the "green revolution" transformed Asian agriculture in the 1970s, making India, Pakistan, and Bangladesh self-sufficient in food. As articulated by 1970 Nobel Peace Prize Laureate agronomist, Norman Borlaug, four ingredients are needed to get a nation's "green revolution" going: *new hybrid seeds, fertilizer, government backing and a free market for the farmers produce.*[15] One or all of these factors have been lacking in Ethiopia at any point in time.

The significance of this study is that while millions of Ethiopians are threatened by horrible and recurrent famines nearly every year, only fifteen percent of its land mass is currently being cultivated as compared to reliable estimates that sixty percent of its land mass has agricultural development potential.[16] Similarly, the country has about three million hectares of potentially irrigable land of which only 150,000 to 200,000 hectares are currently cultivated.[17] This potential agricultural land base could be developed such that Ethiopia could provide adequate food for its own people, as well as export food for the people of other nations. It should be noted that Ethiopia's livestock population is the largest in Africa, and tenth largest in the world, but its contribution to the national economy is very limited. The livestock sub-sector has enormous economic potential. It is most regretful that – given its food production potential – Ethiopia continues to be in a very serious deficit situation with respect to food self-sufficiency and food security.

1.2 What Should be Done

Over the past four decades, there have been numerous studies of Ethiopia's agricultural difficulties and its prospects. A variety of formulas and recipes have been advocated in hope of stimulating faster growth of agricultural output. However, neither the analyses nor the suggested programs have proven to be workable. Too many sound recommendations have been ignored by successive regimes for short-term political reasons. Too many wrong-headed policies have been implemented. Too many smallholder issues remain incompletely explored. Too many proposals failed to take into account the complexity of the real situation faced by small farmers.

A major policy reorientation toward the development of smallholder agriculture clearly is needed. Only by raising the productivity of small farm families who comprise the bulk of the population can food security and sustained broad-based economic growth be attained. Only then can structural transformation – the process whereby Ethiopia's predominately agrarian economy will be transformed into a diversified and productive economy – occur. Rural areas must be given priority for investment in agricultural research, extension, educational, and health institutions, as well as improvements in roads and other physical infrastructure. Equally important is the availability of institutional credit for small farmers, and enriched contacts between change agents and rural people through improved communication strategies, audio-visual productions and mass media presentations. These are needed to improve the quality, impact and outreach of extension messages, and to further involve rural people and their grassroots institutions in the design and execution of development activities in their communities.

To this end, three new developmental dimensions to address the food and agricultural problem and rural poverty are proposed in this study. These are: *a more rational lending policy where poor farmers and peasants would have relatively greater access to farm credit facilities*; *creation of an environment where rural people would actively participate in taking the initiative in decision-making to better control development activities in their communities*; and *increased attention* to *development support communication for motivation, dissemination of technological information and participation in decision-making.*

1.3 This Study

The purpose of this study is twofold. First, it is to study the modern experience of Ethiopia in addressing its interrelated problems of food insecurity and rural poverty. It provides a critical examination of the socio-economic and political conditions of the feudalistic system of the pre-revolutionary imperial regime, the military junta's 1975 agrarian reform effort and its command economic system's impact on agricultural development, and the current regime's strategies affecting food and agriculture under a more capitalistic system. Second, drawing from the lessons learned in Ethiopia, as well as from other African and Asian countries, it recommends a small farmer-led strategy and interventions that would result in significant increases in food and agricultural productivity, and thereby improve levels of living for Ethiopia's rural populace.

This study is organized into eleven chapters.

Chapter 1 provides a brief overview of the food and agricultural crises in Ethiopia over the past four decades, as well as the content of this study.

In *Chapter 2*, the background and history of famine, population growth, urbanization, environmental degradation, land tenure and agricultural development during pre-revolutionary Ethiopia from 1960 until 1974 are examined.

Chapter 3 discusses the magnitude of rural poverty and its impact on Ethiopia's people.

Chapter 4 deals with the December 1960 attempted coup d'etat during Haile Selassie's reign by officers of the Imperial Body Guard, and its aftermath. Following the attempted coup, the imperial government proclaimed its commitment to accelerate economic development and promote progressive institutional changes. Its policies and the resulting achievements and failures are explored.

Chapter 5 covers the post-imperial period of the military-led government. It begins with the 1974 revolution and ends with the 1991 fall from power of Mengistu Hailemariam. It includes an analysis of the 1975 land reform efforts at rural transformation and the crisis of agricultural production. A critical examination is made of the development strategies and policy failures of the military *junta*.

Chapter 6 deals with the post-Mengistu[18] period, after the Ethiopian Peoples Revolutionary Democratic Front came to power in 1991. The impact of ethnic regionalism, incorporation of new lands in the ethnic regions, and public ownership of land on Ethiopian society is critically analyzed and evaluated. It argues that ethnic politics is destructive of Ethiopian society and militates against sustainable development; that ethnic politics should be replaced by a genuinely democratic and widely acceptable system of governance.

Chapter 7 endeavors to highlight the deteriorating socio-economic situation of African states following independence in the 1960s and 1970s from colonial rule. It reviews the causes of the economic crises in sub-Saharan Africa, and examines agricultural and food problems with particular reference to the most important efforts by multilateral agencies to solve sub-Saharan Africa's food crisis.

Chapter 8 addresses the importance of rural credit for small-scale farmers and small-scale entrepreneurs, including women, to improve their productivity and income. An analysis is made of how the rural poor have in the past been denied credit by lending institutions and how they could participate in future programs.

Chapter 9 discusses the requirement for participatory development, i.e., the need for the rural poor to be directly involved in making decisions that affect their lives, especially with reference to program planning, implementation, evaluation and the sharing of the benefits.

Chapter 10 examines the inter-relationship of development support communication and development, and how development support communication supports rural development through information dissemination and training.

Chapter 11 provides the conclusions of this study, and recommends a strategy and interventions needed to address the problems of food insecurity and rural poverty. Approaches to agricultural and rural development are presented with actions directed at overcoming the continuing crises in Ethiopia.

Sources and Notes

[1] Walter Elkan, *Introduction to Development Economics*, revised second edition, (Prentice Hall Harvester Wheatsheaf, 1993), p. 123.

[2] This study recognizes the impact of drought and bad governance, as well as the importance of physical infrastructure and human and institutional capital to agricultural productivity, but focuses less on these than the other causes of "food availability declines" listed here.

[3] See for example, "African drought – It pours, it never rains," (*The Economist*, April 8, 2000), or "Misery and hunger stalk nomads in Africa", by Andrew England, (The Associated Press, April 11, 2000) and "Horn of Africa Famine Appears to be Averted," by Karl Vick, (*The Washington Post*, September 20, 2000).

[4] World Bank, *World Development Report 1982, World Development Indicators*, (The World Bank Group, Washington, D.C., 1982), p. 110.

World Development Report 1985, World Development Indicators, (The World Bank Group, Washington, D.C., 1985), p. 174.

African Development Indicators 1998/99, (The World Bank Group, Washington, D.C., 1998), p. 6.

[5] World Bank, *African Development Indicators 1998/99*, Ethiopia at a Glance, (The World Bank Group, Washington, D.C., 1998), p. 1.

Ethiopia: Agricultural Sector Review, First Draft, (The World Bank Group, Washington, D.C., 1976), p. 4.

[6] The terms, peasant, smallholder, and small farmer are used more or less interchangeably throughout this study.

[7] The terms, military government, military *junta*, *Derg*, and Mengistu government are used more or less interchangeably throughout this study. Since the change in regimes in 1991, the area cultivated by producer cooperatives and state farms has declined.

[8] There are numerous studies around the world that show the importance of production incentives for tenant farmers.
See Adam Szirman, *Economic and Social Development*, (Prentice Hall, 1997), p. 296.

[9] Ajit Kumar Ghose, "Transforming Feudal Agriculture: Agrarian Change in Ethiopia Since 1974," *Journal of Development Studies*, Volume 22, No. 3 (1985), p. 130.

[10] Ibid, p. 128.

[11] Adam Szirmai, op. cit., p. 298.

[12] For more on the role of small farmers in economic development as perceived by influential scholars and practitioners in the 1970s, see Yujiro Hayami and Vernon W. Ruttan, *Agricultural Development: an International Perspective*, (Johns Hopkins Press, 1971), and Bruce F. Johnston and Peter Kilby, *Agriculture and Structural Transformation: Economic Strategies in Late-Developing Countries*, (Oxford University Press, 1975). For more on African small farmers, see Carl K. Eicher, *Food Security Battles in Sub-Saharan Africa*, (Monograph of a plenary address presented at The VII World Congress for Rural Sociology, Bologna, Italy, June 26–July 2, 1988).

[13] Quoted from John M. Cohen, *Integrated Rural Development, The Ethiopian Experience and the Debate*, (The Scandinavian Institute of African Studies, Uppsala, Sweden, 1987), p. 24.

[14] The importance of increased support for small-scale agriculture in Africa has been stressed by the donor community particularly since the 1970s. The 1986 UN Special Debate on Africa concluded, "providing incentives and help for small-scale agriculture holds out better hope for agricultural advances." See Ben Wisner, *Power and Need in Africa*, (Africa World Press Inc., Trenton, New Jersey, 1989), p. 159.

[15] Norman Borlaug, considered to be father of the "green revolution" in wheat production in Asia, and head of the Sasakawa Global 2000 program, quoted in: *The Economist*, (November 1995), p. 42.

[16] James Pickett, *Economic Development in Ethiopia: Agriculture, the Market and the State*, (Development Centre, Organization for Economic Cooperation and Development, OECD, Paris, 1991), p. 29.

[17] Kassu Illala, Federal Democratic Republic of Ethiopia Deputy Prime Minister for Economic Affairs, "Kassu Illala Paints Optimistic Development Plan for Ethiopia," quoted in Amharic magazine *Efoyta* (Addis Ababa, Ethiopia, March 31, 1998), p. 1.

[18] Ethiopians have a first name and another name, but no last "family" name. Their second name is the first name of their father. Thus the head of the

former military government is correctly addressed as Mengistu, not Hailemariam, who was his father.

Chapter 2

Historical Background

2.1 Perennial Nature of the Food Crisis and Rural Poverty

The socio-economic crises of the 1970s and 1980s are not new phenomena to Ethiopia. It has been afflicted by prolonged and repeated drought and famine throughout its long history. According to Richard Pankhurst, between 1540 and 1752 at least eleven major famines are reported to have occurred.[1] Another major famine claimed the lives of many peasants in the northern part of the country between 1828 and 1829. The great Ethiopian famine of 1888-1892 hit the northern region. Tens of thousands of people perished, as did 90 percent of the cattle. The famine was the result of a rinderpest epidemic triggered by Italian importation of infected cattle through the port of Masawa. The situation was exacerbated by drought and a locust invasion that wiped out what was left of the previous harvest, leaving the country in squalid misery. [2]

In the 1950s and 1960s, the principal socio-economic challenge facing the Ethiopian government was that of generating growth in order to raise the living standards of the Ethiopian people on a sustainable basis. In the 1970s and 1980s, the challenge became that of generating enough growth to ensure the bare survival of the people, the majority of whom were confronted with starvation. The main reason for the dismal performance of the agricultural sector was not only the weather. Structural problems in the economy, and specifically in the agricultural sector, were major contributors. Wrong-headed economic policies; the lack of technology development and transfer systems; very limited credit and marketing services; inadequate physical infrastructure; and traditional land tenure systems were all roadblocks to improving smallholder and therefore overall agricultural sector performance. There was a disproportionate transfer of wealth from the rural to urban areas due to the skewed terms of trade between rural and urban Ethiopia. Government policies favored the relatively few large commercial farmers and provided little incentive for small farmers to increase their productivity. During the imperial era, commercial farmers benefited from various government services, including subsidized production inputs and credit. They were provided scarce foreign exchange for duty-free importation of tractors and machinery and spare parts and fuel. Quite often they marketed their own produce. The large commercial farmers were favored because they had close social and political ties with the governing elites.

"Cheap food" policies in general, and misguided government intervention in the pricing and distribution of agricultural commodities in particular, discouraged small farmers from producing in excess of family consumption requirements for off-farm sale. Such policies and interventions contributed to short-term food shortages on numerous occasions. After the land reform proclamations of 1975, small farmers began withholding grain from the market in a successful effort to drive up prices. This was in response to the military government's price control measures and the introduction of compulsory delivery and sale at low fixed prices. Reducing the incentives to grow food led to reduced food production; the ultimate result was higher food prices and waves of discontent in the urban centers that the "cheap food" policies were intended to avert. By the 1970s and 1980s, Ethiopia had to rely heavily on external assistance in the form of humanitarian aid, with some commercial imports, to feed its rapidly growing population.

2.2 Population Growth

A major factor contributing to the perennial nature of the food crisis and rural poverty was and is the high population growth rate. Ethiopia's total population was estimated at 60 million in 1997. Even at a conservative annual growth rate of three percent, Ethiopia's population will double to 120 million by the year 2021. Ethiopia has the third largest population in Africa, after Egypt and Nigeria. At a three percent annual growth rate, Ethiopia will have to feed millions of new mouths every year. With the population increasing on average of three percent a year, and domestic food production only by approximately two percent per year, population will outstrip food production by one percent per year.[3] This means that Ethiopian farmers must increase their output at a sustained minimum rate of at least four per cent per annum to feed the new mouths, as well as better feed those already below the poverty line. This target will be very difficult to achieve given the constraints noted above. However, if domestic production does not rapidly increase, the only choice for Ethiopia is to import millions of tons of grain a year.[4] Imported food must be purchased with scarce foreign exchange, except that which is granted as food aid. Thus Ethiopia would be obliged to continue increasing food imports in spite of the adverse pressure this would put on its already precarious balance of payments situation. The question is not only how long Ethiopia can keep this up. It is also more fundamentally how can Ethiopia finance its overall development when an ever-mounting proportion of its limited foreign exchange resources must be spent on food imports.

2.3 Urbanization

The situation is immensely complicated by the problems of urbanization. Although over three-quarters of the total population live and work in the rural areas and it is recognized that rural development is the key to the nation's economic growth, the population in the urban areas is growing very rapidly. Reliable information is difficult to come by, but the high population growth rate in cities and towns such as Addis Ababa, Bahir Dar, Dessie, Awasa, and Harar, has been and is very alarming. Ethiopia's cities grew at an average rate of nearly six percent per annum, compared to nearly five percent for all low-income countries, during the decade ending in 1984.[5] Since then Ethiopia's urban growth rate has increased to about ten percent, and today nearly a quarter of Ethiopia's population live in urban areas.

Currently, Addis Ababa, the capital city, alone has a total population of more than four million compared to about one-half million two decades ago. The reasons for the high urban population growth rate are rural-to-urban migration and high fertility rates.

The current high urban growth rate will result in most Ethiopians living in massive urban slums. It will be increasingly difficult for these people to feed, clothe, and shelter themselves, let alone find employment and needed social services. Respect for public institutions will be eroded; first there will be increased crime and violence and then there will be social unrest.[6]

Although people migrate for a variety of reasons, empirical evidence indicates very clearly that the primary factor determining migration is economic betterment. Urban areas have potential for a better life than rural areas. Therefore the rural poor tend to migrate to nearby cities and towns hoping for a better life than that in the countryside. Even if rural-to-urban migration declines, urban areas grow at very high rates due to high population growth rates. Moreover, a large number of mostly famine and drought-stricken people flock to towns and cities in search of food and shelter.

Furthermore, some 500,000 former members of the Ethiopian army, navy and air force, who served their country during the imperial and military regimes, are today languishing without severance pay or employment opportunities in Addis Ababa and other population centers. When the rural-to-urban migrants are added to the ex-military personnel, the country's displaced population problem is enormous, and difficult to address.

With the establishment of new governmental administrative centers, particularly in the south and southwest, and an expansion of coffee production and other economic activities in some regions, new towns are being swollen with rural people. Other major causes of rural-urban migration are the widespread unrest due to inter- and intra-ethnic rivalries, and, above all, armed conflicts between the EPRDF and opposition groups, and between Ethiopia and Eritrea.

Another complicating factor is that, as a result of massive food imports, urban dwellers' food preferences have changed. Traditional crops like sorghum, teff, and millet are gradually being supplemented by imported wheat and wheat products and to a lesser degree by other cereals that are not widely produced in Ethiopia.

2.4 Land Tenure

Before the 1974 revolution, there were five traditional types or systems of land ownership in Ethiopia, each conveying certain rights of the individual to the land. These were kinship or communal (*rist*) land, private land, church (*semon*) land, *maderia* land, and government or crown land. By far the most common was communal land mostly found in the northern provinces – particularly Gojjam, Gondar, Tigray, parts of Wollo and northern Shoa. A brief description of each follows:

Kinship or Communal (Rist) Land

In this system, all descendants (both male and female) of an individual who initially acquired the property were entitled to a share and individuals had the right to use their plots in perpetuity. No user of any piece of land could sell his or her share outside the family or mortgage or bequeath his or her share as a gift, as the land belonged not to the individual but to the descent group.[7] Under this system land could be leased temporarily. Each *rist*-holder paid to the state a fixed annual tribute for the use of the land in his possession. In general, absentee landlordism in the north was rare and there were few landless tenants. The vast majority of the peasants in these areas worked parcels of land that increasingly diminished in size due to continued fragmentation. The Third Five-Year Development Plan drafted in 1968 made the point that 90 percent of the peasant farmers had less than five hectares each and that 66 percent farmed less than half a hectare.[8]

Private Land

This type of ownership existed in the southern provinces. Here land ownership was concentrated in a relatively small number of hands. The majority of the peasantry was tenant farmers and sharecroppers. It is estimated that one-third of the total cropland was tenant-operated as shown in Table 1.

TABLE 1
DISTRIBUTION OF AGRICULTURAL HOLDINGS AND
CROPLAND BY SYSTEM OF TENURE

Tenure System	Total Holdings (%)	Total Cropland (%)
Communal	11	6
Owner-Operated	38	37
Tenant-Operated	36	33
Owned & Rented (Mixed)	15	24

Source: *Agricultural Sample Survey, 1974/75, Volume 1*, Ministry of Agriculture, Addis Ababa, July 19, 1975, p. 60

According to the 1974/75 Agricultural Sample Survey, over one-third of the total agricultural land holdings in the country, and just one-third of the country's cropland were operated by tenant cultivators. On the other hand, owner-operated holdings were 38 percent of total holdings and 37 percent of total cropland. Thus owner-operated holdings and cropland were about the same as tenant-operated holdings and cropland. When the "mixed" tenure system is combined with owner-operated and tenant-operated holdings, the above percentages are significantly increased.

The majority of the peasantry had access to land, but this accessibility was acquired at a heavy price – the loss of the major portion of its produce, dependency, and burdensome economic and extra-economic obligation.[9] Article 2991 of the 1960 Civil Code permitted the landowner to take from the tenant as much as 75 percent of the latter's produce, although in practice such crop-sharing arrangements were virtually unknown. The most common form of paying rent was sharecropping. The share paid varied between one-third and one-half of the harvest. In addition to rent, the tenant put aside one-tenth of his crop to cover the landlord's tithe (one-tenth), even after the tithe had been legally abolished in 1967. Most of the tenants supplied their oxen, plows, and seeds; in this case the most common rent was one-third of the crop. In general, lease agreements between landowners and tenants were oral, creating insecurity of tenure. Tenants were not, as a rule, compensated for the permanent improvements they had made on the holdings. On the contrary, if a tenant increased the value of the holding by permanent improvements, the landowner often responded by increasing the rent. Eviction of tenants without good reason and without notice of termination was very common. The situation described above varied from province to province and even from district to district. The tenants in the south were the most impoverished and least powerful group of people in the rural areas.

Church (Semon) Land

Other forms of tenure included church or *semon* land that was possessed by the Ethiopian Orthodox Church. This was land the government had granted to the Ethiopian Orthodox Church in perpetuity. The amount of land owned by the church or actual revenue generated from it is not accurately known. Traditionally, the church claimed that about one-third of Ethiopia's land was *semon* land, but Dessalegn Rahmato estimates it was not more than ten percent of the agricultural land of the country.[10] The church depended on income from the land to support its missionary activities and to pay salaries to its 170,000 clergy and church functionaries. Peasants who worked on church land paid tribute to the church (monastery) rather than to the state. The church lost all its land after the 1974 revolution.

Maderia Land
Maderia was that land given to low-ranking and other government employees in lieu of salary or pension. Normally this grant was temporary, valid only over the period the individual held office, but it could also be for life. The State owned large tracts of agricultural land known as *maderia* and *mengist*. *Mengist* was land registered as government property, and *maderia* was land granted mainly to government officials, war veterans and other patriots in lieu of a pension, or salary.

Crown Land
The crown also held land of its own, known as crown land. This land was farmed by tenants who in return were given land for their own use, usually under terms of temporary tenure. By 1974, about 47 percent of the total land of Ethiopia could be classified as crown land. This was about 12 percent of all arable land.

Nomadic and Pastoral Lands
The nomadic and pastoral lands are located in the lowland periphery and the Great Rift Valley. The people living in the lowland periphery (below 1500 meters) are nomadic, relying solely upon the rearing of livestock for their livelihood. The nomadic and pastoral people's social structure is based on a kinship system with strong inter-clan connections; grazing and water rights are regulated by custom. The nomadic and pastoral lands have not been affected by the 1975 land reform proclamation that made all rural lands the collective property of all Ethiopians.

2.5 Environmental Degradation

Ethiopia has been subjected to extreme ecological disaster and environmental degradation, especially in terms of the loss of valuable soil, forest and general vegetative cover. This has now reached alarming levels. Ethiopia's deforestation has actually contributed much to its climate change, increasing the frequency of drought. The 1970/71 Central Statistical Office Survey classified some eleven percent of Ethiopia's total land area as cultivated land, 54 percent as pasture, ten percent as rivers and lakes, seven percent as forests, four percent as swamps and fourteen percent as barren land.[11] In Ethiopia, the total land covered by forests has declined from 40 percent to less than three percent in a period of 70 years.[12]

This information alone spells looming catastrophe for a country that relies on wood for 90 per cent of its fuel, and whose population is likely to quadruple within 48 years. The demand for firewood and timber are the two principal causes behind the deforestation activity. Land clearing for farmland and grazing and recurring droughts have contributed to the depletion of the forestry resource.

Land tenure has been and is a major contributor to the failure of reforestation efforts. Prior to 1974, the government failed to implement widespread conservation measures, largely because the country's complex land tenure system stymied efforts to halt soil erosion and improve the land.[13] Following nationalization of rural lands in 1975, overgrazing, intensive cultivation, and deforestation of slopes not suited to agriculture have eroded the soil, a situation that worsened considerably during the 1970s and 1980s. The 1975 land reform proclamations gave farmers only usufruct (use) rights to the land. This type of tenure arrangement gave rise to indifference to sustaining the quality and durability of the soil. The general sentiment was that the right to use the land could be taken away at any time; therefore, why spend money and effort to keep it productive. This uncertainty stems from the land tenure policy pursued by the government and from the various contradictory administrative orders rural people were asked to follow.

As pointed out earlier, the Ethiopia highlands suffer from massive land degradation due to soil erosion. If this degradation continues, eighteen percent of the highland will be bare rock by the year 2010 and ten million people will not be able to produce food from the land.[14] In particular, the degradation of potential cropland poses serious difficulties. Degraded soil is unfertile and makes less water available for plant use due to high surface runoff or contamination. Once the soil is severely degraded, the investment needed to rehabilitate it can be exorbitant. In 1978, a report circulating in the United States Embassy in Addis Ababa pointed out that about one billion tons of topsoil was eroded annually from the Ethiopian highlands.[15]

The 1975 agrarian reform proclamation abolished private ownership of forests. Forests covering more than 80 hectares were placed under the jurisdiction of the government's State Forestry Development Department, while smaller plots were to be administered by the peasant associations. These newly formed associations were suddenly entrusted with power without having any guidelines for managing forest resources. In addition, they had neither the institutional capacity nor the manpower to manage forest resources.[16] The other stumbling block was the insecurity of tree ownership. Without the legal right to own the trees, success in forest projects was unlikely.

Sources and Notes

[1] Mesfin Woldemariam, *Rural Vulnerability to Famines in Ethiopia: 1958-1977*, (New Delhi, Vikas Publishing House, 1984), p. 31.

[2] Richard K. Pankhurst, "The Great Ethiopian Famine of 1888-1892: a new assessment," *The Journal of the History of Medicine and Allied Sciences*, (1966), p. 95-124, 271-294.

Bahru Zewde, *A History of Modern Ethiopia, 1855-1974*, Eastern African Studies, (James Currey Ltd., London, Ohio University Press, Athens, and Addis Ababa University Press, Addis Ababa, 1991), p. 72.

[3] World Bank, *African Development Indicators 1998/99*, (World Bank Group, Washington, D.C., 1998), p. 7.

Ethiopia's agricultural output increased 2.3 per cent per annum from 1987 through 1997.

[4] *The Economist*, quote from Food and Agricultural Organization (FAO) report (November 25, 1995), p. 5.

[5] Mulatu Wubneh and Yohannis Abate, *Ethiopia: Transition and Development in the Horn of Africa*, (Westview Press, Boulder, Colorado, 1988), p. 138.

[6] Kinfe Abraham, *The Missing Millions: Why and How Africa is Underdeveloped*, (Africa World Press Inc., Trenton, New Jersey, 1995), p. 269.

[7] For further elaboration of this system see Thomas P. Ofcansky and LaVerle Berry, Editors, *Ethiopia: A Country Study, 4th Edition*, (Federal Research Division, Library of Congress, Government Printing Office, Washington, D.C., 1993), p. 166.

[8] Patrick Gilkes, *The Dying Lion, Feudalism and Modernization*, (Julian Friedmann Ltd, International Press Centre, Shoe Lane, England, UK, 1975), p. 121.

[9] Dessalegn Rahmato, "The Ethiopian Experience in Agrarian Reform," in *Challenging Rural Poverty*, edited by Fassil G. Kiros, (Africa World Press Inc., Trenton, New Jersey, 1983), p. 203.

[10] Ibid. p. 199.

[11] Michael Stahl, *Ethiopia: Political Contradictions in Agricultural Development*, (Liber Tryck, Stockholm, 1974), p. 79.

[12] Kinfe Abraham, op. cit., p. 24.

[13] Refer for instance to Thomas P. Ofcansky and LaVerle Berry, op. cit., p. 166.

[14] Alemneh Dejene, *Environment, Famine, and Politics in Ethiopia: A View from the Village*, (Lynne Rienner, Boulder, Colorado, 1990), p. 96.

---

[15] Cited by Samuel M. Murithi in *"African Development Dilemma,"* (University Press of America, Inc., Lanham, New York and London, 1996), p. 39.

[16] Alemneh Dejene, op. cit., p. 7.

Chapter 3

Rural Poverty

3.1 The Poverty Problem

Ethiopia is one of the poorest countries in the world. Its per capita GNP in 1997 was only $US110, among the lowest in the world. The GNP in 1997 for sub-Saharan Africa was US$500, and in low-income countries worldwide it was US$350. Poverty and economic retardation has become a permanent state for the majority of Ethiopians. Life expectancy is 50 years. The infant mortality rate is 107 per 1,000 live births and 48 percent of children under 5 years of age are malnourished or weigh less than acceptable standards for their age. The population growth noted in Chapter 2 absorbs most gains in economic growth and seriously impairs improving nutrition, education, and health care. It also contributes to severe ecological degradation. Perhaps as many as thirty million of Ethiopia's 60 million people live below the national poverty line, subsisting on less than one US dollar per day.[1]

Those living below the national poverty line are considered to be living in "absolute poverty." This is defined as a condition in which it is not possible to obtain the basic needs of life or where deprivation is so severe that the basic needs of life can scarcely be met. It is the minimum level required for survival.[2] It is further defined in terms of high malnutrition and infant mortality rates, inadequate housing and pervasive illiteracy. Where basic needs are not met, the effect on human beings can be devastating. Estimates on the incidence of poverty may vary depending on the methodology used in making such estimates. Nonetheless, there is general agreement that the incidence of rural poverty in Ethiopia is one of the highest in Africa and in the world.

As the percentage of poor people in Ethiopia's rural areas is higher than the percentage of the poor in urban centers, the incidence of "rural" poverty is higher than the combined "rural and urban" poverty level estimates for the whole country. Nearly all of Ethiopia's rural poor are subsistence small farm families engaged in food production for home consumption. They are the most disadvantaged group of people in Ethiopia.

A small percentage of the labor force also works for wages in urban centers. The living standard for this group is slightly better than for those in the rural areas. Since 1985, a minimum wage has been set and paid to public sector employees who are by far the largest group of wage earners. The public sector minimum monthly wage is now US$16.80 (105 Ethiopian *birr*). This does not provide an adequate standard of living for a worker and family. A family of five requires a monthly income of US$62.40 (390 Ethiopian *birr*). Thus even with two minimum wage earners, a family receives only about half of the income needed for subsistence. Furthermore, periodic price increases adversely affect urban wage earners on fixed incomes as most of their pay is spent on food and shelter. The government enacted wage freezes after the 1974 revolution and low starting wages and salaries made it difficult, if not impossible, for urban wage earners to improve their living standard. Real wages for Ethiopian agricultural workers fell by nearly 20 percent between 1974 and 1985. This means that the living standards of agricultural wage earners declined 30 percent. [3]

3.2 The Food-Population Equation

As discussed in Chapter 2, a major cause of increasing poverty has been Ethiopia's high population growth rate. It has severely out-stripped agricultural production, as shown in Table 2.

TABLE 2
AGRICULTURAL PRODUCTION INCREASE AND
POPULATION GROWTH RATE (%): 1965-1997

Years	Agricultural Production	Population
1965-1973	2.1	2.6
1974-1979	0.6	2.6
1980-1987	-2.1	2.4
1988-1997	2.3	3.2

Sources: The World Bank *Area Handbook Series, Ethiopia: A Country Study*, 1993, and The World Bank, *African Development Indicators 1998/99*, October 1998.

As Table 2 indicates, during the 32-year period food production has registered a very low or negative growth rate. The gap between the food production and population growth rates increased from 0.5 percent to 5.5 percent, but in recent years has narrowed to 0.9 percent.

As discussed in Chapters 1 and 2, the poor performance of agriculture also has been the result of the unstable political climate with wrong-headed government policies, and drought. The unstable political climate and bad policies contributed in general to the overall low levels of productivity of the dominant small farm sector.

3.3 The Human Development Index

Since 1990, the United Nations Development Program (UNDP) has published annually a global assessment of human progress known as the *Human Development Index (HDI) Report*. It is an assessment of human progress as measured by educational attainment, life expectancy at birth, food and nutrition, and adjusted real income. The reports rank countries as high, medium or low based on these indicators. The 1999 HDI Report[4] reveals the following:

Of the 174 countries included in the assessment, 45 are in the high human development category, 94 in the medium category, and 35 in the low category. Canada, the United States, and Norway are at the top of the HDI. Sierra Leone, Niger and Ethiopia are at the bottom of the HDI. African countries in the medium category include South Africa, Tunisia, Algeria, Swaziland, Egypt, Botswana, Lesotho, Zimbabwe, Ghana, Cameroon, Congo and Kenya.

The HDI is used to estimate the quality of life of nations and ranks them accordingly. It is also a partial measurement of poverty as it includes several indices that are meaningful indicators of poverty levels. However it does not include measures of political and cultural deprivation. [5]

Table 3 compares several social indicators used in the HDI for Ethiopia and selected countries. It depicts a gloomy and alarming picture of poverty in Ethiopia.

TABLE 3
SOCIAL INDICATORS FOR ETHIOPIA AND SELECTED COUNTRIES
Percent of Population with Access to:

	Health Services	Safe Water	Sanitation	Per Capita Daily Calorie Supply (2100 = minimum requirement)	Life Expectancy at Birth	Adult Literacy Rate (%)	Real GDP Per Capita (US$)	Under-Weight Children Under Five (% of Total Population)
Ethiopia	**55**	**25**	**19**	**1,845**	**43.3**	**35.4**	**510**	**48**
Bangladesh	74	95	43	2,105	58.1	38.9	1,050	56
Burundi	80	52	51	1,708	42.4	44.6	630	37
Hong Kong	99	100	100	3,202	78.2	92.4	24,350	---
Mauritius	100	97	99	2,952	71.4	83.0	9,310	16
Sudan	51	48	75	2,391	55.0	42.7	1,560	34
Mexico	82	93	83	3,137	72.2	90.0	8,370	7

Source: Extracted from the *UNDP Annual Human Development Index: 1999.*

Among the countries listed in Table 3, Ethiopia, Bangladesh, Burundi and the Sudan were selected randomly from the "low human development" category. Mauritius was chosen as evidence that high achievement is possible for a multi-ethnic, multi-lingual African nation. Mexico and Hong Kong are included as examples of "medium" and "high" categories.

3.4 Health and Nutrition

As the UNDP and other poverty studies indicate, Ethiopia is at the bottom on the scale of human progress and development. The health and nutritional data are most revealing. The great majority of Ethiopians are exposed to often rampant and fatal diseases and malnutrition. As noted in Table 3, only 55 percent of the population has access to health services. And there are wide disparities between rural and urban, and from region to region. Only 25 percent of the population has access to safe drinking water compared to an average of 60 percent for other developing countries. The level of sanitation is equally pathetic. Only 19 percent have access to proper sanitation facilities compared to 36 percent for Africa as a whole.[6] The combination of inadequate water supply and limited sanitation is a guaranteed recipe for the rapid spread of water-born diseases. Clean water and sanitation are necessary basic human needs. These are not luxuries.

The incidence of undernourishment is most prevalent and most severe. While the standard per capita daily calorie requirement is 2100, the average daily intake for Ethiopians is only 1845 calories. As Assefa Negesh rightly noted, until recently the majority of Ethiopians could not even find two-thirds of the minimum daily caloric intake needed for the normal physiological functioning of a human being.[7] These conditions are clearly a reflection of the low level of the quantity and quality of food consumed. The prevalence of malnutrition in children under five years of age was very high at 48 percent in 1997.[8] Ethiopia registers the worst maternal mortality rate in the world. According to Assefa Negesh, 40,000 mothers die annually during childbirth.[9] In 1997, the adult literacy rate in Ethiopia stood at 35 percent compared to 57 percent for sub-Saharan Africa and 53 percent for low-income countries worldwide. Also in 1997, life expectancy at birth in Ethiopia was 43 years, compared to 52 years for sub-Saharan Africa and 59 years for low-income countries worldwide.[10] Females have a much higher illiteracy rate than males. Development programs are most difficult to implement when developers must deal with predominantly illiterate peasant communities. As Howard Handelman states, "democracy is difficult to achieve unless a country has crossed a threshold of 50 percent literacy."[11]

Due to the lack of vitamin A, one percent of the country's population is blind. In 1984, the population per physician was 78,770 compared to all low-income developing countries where one physician served 5,890 patients.[12] Malnutrition and diarrhea-causing diseases account for most of child mortality. Ethiopian babies face a critical diaper shortage; 2000 Ethiopian mothers find themselves competing daily for 1200 maternity beds. The average hospital stay for the 50 percent of Ethiopian women who deliver in hospitals is twelve hours and women planning a cesarean section must bring their own thread for the surgery.[13]

Ethiopia is one of the nations hardest hit by the HIV epidemic, although this has not been widely reported in the international news media. Out of its population of 60 million, eleven percent or over six million are known to be HIV infected.[14] The HIV infection is most common among the most economically productive age group, 15 to 35. About 100 persons die daily from HIV-related diseases particularly in the cities and other population centers. More evidence is available that suggests that HIV has infected a large number of children and women, as well as men, but to date little attention has been given to ameliorate this situation.

During the *Derg* era, the number one killer of youth was the so-called "Red Terror." It was responsible for the death of an estimated 40,000 young Ethiopians. Under the EPRDF regime, it is malaria, tuberculosis, HIV/AIDS, and ethnic cleansing. It is with good reason that Ethiopians fear that agricultural production will be negatively affected unless serious measures are taken to control the spread of HIV.

3.5 Other Indicators of Poverty

Ethiopia has one of the world's lowest per capita GNP figures. As indicated above, the World Bank estimated per capita GNP in 1997 at US$110. It is clear that the majority of Ethiopians live in the midst of a vicious cycle of poverty and despair with inadequate access to the necessities of life that citizens of most nations take for granted. Thus far we have discussed the causes and magnitude of poverty in Ethiopia. Now let us go one step further and illustrate how the low level of expenditures in the social sectors has deepened rural poverty.

Table 4 shows central government expenditures by function as a percentage of total public expenditures in selected African countries.

TABLE 4
CENTRAL GOVERNMENT EXPENDITURES IN SELECTED
AFRICAN COUNTRIES: 1991-1995
(AS A PERCENTAGE OF TOTAL PUBLIC EXPENDITURES)

	Health	*Education*	*Social Security & Welfare*	*Defense*
Ethiopia	**4.2**	**12.4**	**5.8**	**30.2**
Cameroon	4.8	18.0	1.0	9.4
Egypt	2.4	12.0	10.4	9.4
Ghana	7.8	23.0	7.0	4.7
Kenya	5.6	20.3	0.1	7.6

Source: The World Bank, *World Development Report 1997*, (Oxford University Press, June 1997).

National governments' levels of commitment to social objectives can be measured and compared by observing the percentage of their total budget expenditures invested in the social sectors. Although Ethiopian government investment in the social sectors has increased in recent years in absolute terms, it has not markedly improved as a percentage of total budget expenditures. This is a result of the large proportion of the total budget expended in support of the military. It is ironic that 1992 defense expenditures were US$881 million, almost double the 1985 defense expenditures of US$447 million. In 1992, Ethiopia spent over 20 percent of its GDP/GNP for national defense when the vital interest of the nation was not at stake.[15] In the table above, note the low percentage of defense expenditures of the other countries compared to Ethiopia. Also note the higher percentage of social sector expenditures of other countries compared to Ethiopia. It is little wonder that health and educational levels in Ethiopia remain very low.

Table 5 provides an assessment of the incidence of rural poverty in Africa for the period 1970-80. Since that time, comparable assessments of the incidence of rural poverty in Ethiopia have not been published.

TABLE 5
INCIDENCE OF ABSOLUTE RURAL POVERTY
IN AFRICA: 1970-1980
(Percentage Based on Estimated Poverty Line for Each Country)

Ethiopia	65	Lesotho	55
Rwanda	90	Botswana	55
Malawi	85	Zambia	52
Burundi	85	Nigeria	51
Zaire	80	Madagascar	50
Somalia	70	Swaziland	50
Sierra Leone	65	Mali	48
Benin	65	Cameroon	40
Tanzania	60	Gambia	40
Chad	56	Niger	35
Ghana	55	Mauritius	12
Kenya	55		

Source: FAO, *Development Strategies for the Rural Poor, Economic and Social Development, Paper 44*, (Rome, Italy, 1984), p. 92.

The estimates show relatively low rural poverty in Mauritius at 12 percent. Rural poverty in Rwanda and Malawi were very high at 90 percent and 85 percent respectively. Ethiopia was relatively high at 65 percent. However, knowledgeable observers report that poverty in Ethiopia has greatly increased since 1980 vis-à-vis other African countries. Currently some eleven million Ethiopians are at risk of starvation.[16]

As noted above, subsistence agriculture dominates the Ethiopian economy. Some 85 percent of its people must produce food in order to survive. The small farm, peasant family is a nearly self-contained unit of production and consumption. It has little capital. Land ownership is not individualized. Over 60 percent farm less than one hectare. With many small fragmented plots the rural labor force is not used effectively. Only about a third of the able working-age males work full-time. More than half are without work part of the year, mostly during the harvest and major rainy season from June through September. Credit is hard to obtain, markets are underdeveloped and risks are high for households living at the subsistence level. They are unable to invest in new agricultural production technology, e.g., improved seed, fertilizer, pesticides, and irrigation. Less than fourteen percent of small farmers use fertilizer, no more than two percent use improved seeds, less than five percent use herbicides and fewer than one percent use pesticides. Irrigation is available to less than five percent of all farmers.[17]

Those familiar with Ethiopia believe that many Ethiopians are still starving to death every year. While the precise number of deaths due to starvation is difficult to establish, Mesfin Wolde-Mariam estimates that in the 20 years between 1958 and 1977, a minimum of two and possibly up to five million people died; a death rate of between 100,000 and 250,000 per annum.[18] The number of people affected by famine since the mid-1970s is even more alarming. According to Fassil Kiros, some 58 million people were affected by famine between 1973 and 1986. He further argues that nearly 4 million people are debilitated every year because their basic human needs are not being met.[19]

The 1948 *United Nations Universal Declaration of Human Rights* is quite explicit about basic human needs:

> Everyone has the right to a standard of living adequate for the health and well being of himself and his family, including food and clothing, housing and medical care and necessary social services, and the right to security in the event of unemployment, sickness, disability, widowed, old age or lack of livelihood in circumstances beyond his control.[20]

Sources and Notes

[1] World Bank, "Ethiopia at a glance," in *African Development Indicators 1998/99*, (World Bank Group, Washington, D.C., 1998).

[2] Jossy R. Bibangambah, "Approaches to the Problem of Rural Poverty in Africa," in *Challenging Rural Poverty*, edited by Fassil G. Kiros, (Africa World Press Inc., Trenton, New Jersey, 1985), p. 24-33.

[3] John Markakis and Nega Ayele, *Class and Contradiction in Ethiopia*, (The Red Sea Press, Trenton, New Jersey, 1986), p. 142-143.

Thomas P. Ofcansky and LaVerle Berry, Editors, *Ethiopia: A Country Study, 4th Edition*, (Federal Research Division, Library of Congress, Government Printing Office, Washington, D.C., 1993), p. 162.

[4] United Nations Development Program (UNDP), *Annual Human Development Report: 1999*, (Oxford University Press, New York and London, 1999).

[5] Lual A. Deng, *Rethinking African Development: Toward a Framework for Social Integration and Ecological Harmony*, (African World Press Inc., Trenton, New Jersey, 1998), p. 105.

[6] UNDP 1999, Table 3, and World Bank 1998, op. cit.

[7] Assefa Negesh, *The Pillage of Ethiopia by Eritreans and Their Tigrean Surrogates,* (Adey Publishing Company, Los Angeles, California, 1996), p. 111.

[8] UNDP 1999, Table 3, and World Bank 1998, op. cit.

[9] Assefa Negesh, op. cit., p. 111.

[10] UNDP 1999, Table 3, and World Bank 1998, op. cit.

[11] Howard Handelman, *The Challenge of THIRD WORLD Development,* (Prentice Hall, Upper Saddle River, New Jersey), p. 248.

[12] World Bank, *World Development Report 1991-The Challenge of Development,* (Oxford University Press, 1991), p. 258.

[13] Information provided to the author by a reliable Ethiopian Ministry of Health official.

[14] UNAIDS, "World Bank is Targeting AIDS in Africa," People ages 15-49 in selected countries, 1999 data, from article in (*Wall Street Journal,* September 12, 2000).

[15] Selamawit Gerimu, "What is the Economic Situation in Ethiopia?" *The Ethiopian Register,* (Avon, Minnesota, September 1995), p. 25.

[16] World Bank, 1998, op. cit. In mid-2000, some 8-10.5 million Ethiopians were at risk of starvation in southeastern Ethiopia. See, for example, "African drought – It pours, it never rains," (*The Economist,* April 8, 2000), or "Misery and hunger stalk nomads in Africa," by Andrew England, (The Associated Press, April 11, 2000) and "Horn of Africa Famine Appears to be Averted," by Karl Vick, (*The Washington Post,* September 20,2000).

[17] James Pickett, *Economic Development in Ethiopia: Agriculture, the Market and the State,* (Organisation for Economic Co-operation and Development, OECD Development Centre, Paris, 1991), p. 15.

[18] Mesfin Wolde-Mariam, cited by Fassil G. Kiros in *The Subsistence Crisis in Africa: The Case of Ethiopia,* (Organization for Social Science Research in Eastern Africa, Nairobi, Kenya, 1993), p. 7.

[19] Fassil G. Kiros, *The Subsistence Crisis in Africa: The Case of Ethiopia,* (Organization for Social Science Research in Eastern Africa, 1993), p. 7.

[20] Ben Wisner, *Power and Need in Africa,* (Africa World Press Inc., Trenton, New Jersey, 1989), p. 25.

Chapter 4

The 1960 Abortive *Coup D'etat* and its Aftermath

4.1 Land Reform

On December 13,1960, while Emperor Haile Selassie was on a state visit to Brazil there was an attempted *coup d'etat* led by General Mengistu Neway, Commander of the Imperial Body Guard and some civilian intellectuals led by his younger brother, Germame Neway. As Keller argues, the *coup* was important not so much for what it achieved, but because it ushered in a rising protest over Ethiopia's distorted development strategy that culminated in the successful *coup* of 1974.[1] Although the attempted *coup* was unsuccessful, it was a real turning point in the history of the country. As Daniel Teferra aptly explains, "It opened a new chapter in the political history of Ethiopia by creating political awareness in the minds of the people and suggesting a modern political process as an alternative to the traditional order."[2] John Harbeson also argues, "The *coup* attempt was a warning to the Emperor that the pressure for economic and social changes were beginning to outrun measures introduced by his regime in the name of progressive change."[3] The *coup* leaders did not mention land reform by name, perhaps for tactical reasons. Nonetheless, Germame Neway, the architect of the *coup*, believed that Ethiopia's economic stagnation could be broken, " . . . only by the full participation of a population freed from exploitation and permitted under wise leadership to act in its own self-interest."[4] As governor of Walayta *Awraja* (district), Germame made efforts to ease the burden of the poorest by distributing unused land to landless and unemployed peasants. By introducing a written lease agreement between tenants and landlords, he was able to discourage tenant eviction by landlords. Germame always spoke out about the plight of the poor and the deprived. He was the moving spirit behind the attempted *coup*. General Mengistu, on the other hand, did not hesitate to mention to university students the social progress achieved by the newly independent African States in comparison to Ethiopia. He noted that, even though Ethiopia was the only country in Africa never colonized, its lack of social progress was very embarrassing.

On December 15th, the late Crown Prince Asfa Wossen, who was intended to be the future constitutional monarch, made an oblique reference to land reform in a radio address to the nation. In that address he stated:

> From this day onward, every person will be given land according to his needs and will be able to live in peace. Moreover, those whose land has been taken away for a variety of reasons had but a little money cast in their direction. By returning this money, they will from now on be entitled to take back their lands.[5]

The Crown Prince did not raise the fundamental question of land reform in this address. It is an open question whether the *coup* leaders would have undertaken land reform in the wake of the *coup* or, if they did, what kind of land reform would have ensued. One tenet the *coup* leaders repeatedly pledged and promised was restoration of Ethiopia to its former glory.[6]

In any event, as the other units of the armed forces, particularly the army and the air force, were not consulted about the planned *coup*, Mengistu and his supporters were badly defeated. The Emperor returned to Addis Ababa on December 17th to find the loyalists in full control. Haile Selassie did not understand that the root cause of the failed *coup d'etat* was general dissatisfaction with the lack of social and economic progress in the country. Nor did he appreciate the role and significance of land reform in social and economic progress. In his refusal to acknowledge the need for reform, he sought to blame the *coup* on the evil intentions of a small section of the armed forces. In the words of Harold Marcus, "the Emperor refused to acknowledge the need for reform and attributed the *coup* to a small group of willful men whose action had shamed Ethiopia."[7] From 1960 on, however, rather than being able to dictate comfortably the rate and direction of change, the Emperor was placed ever more on the defensive, having to work harder to mediate the demands of increasingly politically significant social groupings.[8] Even though Haile Selassie returned to Addis Ababa triumphantly, no sooner had he arrived at his capital than rumors of another *coup* by a different unit of the army started circulating in the city. Fear and anxiety gripped the imperial family. The Emperor was advised that it was necessary to implement some kind of reforms to stabilize the fragile political situation and gain public confidence.

Soon thereafter, in February 1961, the Emperor unexpectedly appointed 58 officials to key positions in the government.[9] These were men who in the past had demonstrated their personal loyalty to the Emperor. He also unexpectedly appointed a high-level Land Reform Committee under the chairmanship of Colonel Tamrat Yigezu, then Minister of Community Development and a close confidant of the Emperor. The Land Reform Committee included Yilma Deresa, Minister of Finance; Belete Gabre Tsadique, Vice-Minister of Agriculture and later Minister of Land Reform and Administration; Solomon Abraham, Vice-Minister of Interior; Worku Habtewolde, Head of the Planning Commission; Like Seltanat Habtemariam Workneh, now Abuna Melkesedek, Archbishop of the Ethiopian Orthodox Church; and Dejazmach Kebede Tessema, Head of the Territorial Army. The committee chairman approached the Food and Agriculture Organization (FAO) to provide experts on land administration and land tenure. Subsequently, Chairman Tamrat was transferred to Gondar province as Governor, and the chairmanship went to Akale Work Habtewolde, elder brother of Prime Minister Aklilu Habtewolde.

In 1962 the two FAO experts, Mr. J.C.D. Lawrence, and Dr. H.S. Mann arrived in Ethiopia. They were joined later by this author who served as counterpart and secretary to the Land Reform Committee. As discussed below, some of the imperial reforms were clearly prompted by the abortive *coup* of 1960.[10] The first challenge of the UN experts was to conduct systematic nationwide land tenure studies and to evaluate the tenure situation in order to formulate appropriate policy recommendations. Prior to the 1974 revolution, Ethiopia had one of the most complex land tenure systems in the world. Wollo province alone had 111 types of land tenure. Meanwhile, the Second Five-Year Development Plan (1963-68) had already proposed implementation of programs dealing with landlord-tenant relations, progressive land taxation, abolition of out-of-date holdings, and cadastral survey and registration. The Five Year Plan did not, however, include provision for

1. Emperor Haile Selassie

2. Prime Minister Aklilu Habtewolde

3. Akale Work Habtewolde, Minister of Agriculture and Land
Reform Committee Chairman

4. Belete Gabre Tsadique, First Minister of Land Reform and
Administration

a budget or an organization to implement the plan. In 1964, the two FAO experts submitted the Land Policy Project to the Land Reform Committee. It contained, *inter alia*, the organizational structure for a new Ministry of Land Reform and Administration, its budgetary and manpower requirements, and a plan for operation. Other administrative recommendations involved transferring landlord-tenant relations to the new ministry from the Ministry of Agriculture; land classification from the Ministry of Finance; and land survey, registration, and distribution from the Ministry of Interior. Also the Mapping and Geography Institute, which had been a separate entity, was to become one of the departments of the new ministry.

In the same year, draft legislation on tenancy was presented to Parliament. However, it was rejected by both houses. The draft legislation was concerned with improvements in the legal status of the tenant farmer. The aim of the bill was to encourage landlords and tenants to recognize each other's rights and obligations, and to cooperate in increasing agricultural productivity that would contribute to the future prosperity of Ethiopia. Its main provisions were:

Land leases were to be written or oral – in most cases there were no written agreements prior to this draft law. Either party could require that the lease be in writing. In some instances, the initiative could come from the Minister of Land Reform and Administration.

The rent, which could be paid either in cash or kind, was to be limited to one-third of the crop harvest in the case of sharecropping. If the landlord contributed some of the variable inputs, such as seed or oxen, he could obtain more than one-third, providing that the total did not exceed one-half of the harvest.

Rents were to be converted to a fixed amount or to cash based on the calculation that the amount of produce equal to one-third of the crop harvest is considered as the fixed rent.

Tenancies were to be terminated at the agreement of both parties or by the initiative of either. The tenant could terminate the relationship by giving a one-year notice to the landowner of his intentions.

Compensation was to be provided for improvements whatever the reason for terminating the tenancy, and the amount was to be equal to the unexhausted value of the improvement.

If the landholder intended to sell the holding, the tenant cultivating it would be given the right of pre-emption at a reasonable price. [11]

The above proclamation did not abolish sharecropping that would have greatly benefited tenant farmers. Similarly, the provision for illegal eviction of a tenant had some loopholes that could undermine the tenant's position *vis-à-vis* the landlord.

In 1965 University College Students Union of Addis Ababa demonstrated before Parliament carrying banners with the slogan, "land to the tiller." In subsequent years, this slogan proved to be one of the driving forces for political and social change. One of the FAO experts resigned from his post in late 1964, the stated reason being because progress in land reform was very slow and piecemeal.

In 1968, three pieces of legislation were presented to Parliament that dealt with agricultural tenancy, registration of agricultural land, and taxation of unutilized land. The French-educated Prime Minister, Aklilu Habtewolde, who came from a poor family background, was in favor of meaningful land reform in Ethiopia, but he faced stiff opposition in his own Cabinet. The most conservative members of the Council of Ministers argued for distribution of government land to landless people rather than regulating tenancy. Others argued that the draft legislation did not go far enough, and still others did not see the need for any land reform program. The majority of the ministers were handpicked by the Emperor himself from among the Shoa nobility. The appointment of Belete Gabre Tsadique in 1966 as the first Minister of Land Reform and Administration had brought about a rise in hope among pro-reform individuals and advocates. Belete Gabre Tsadique had made it clear that further delay in implementing land reform measures would create mass upheavals that the country had never seen before. Unfortunately, his efforts not only failed, but also lost his job as a consequence.[12] He was then immediately transferred to Moscow as the new Ethiopian Ambassador to that country. Christopher Clapham was dead right when he wrote, "Ambassadorships were a common form of comfortable exile."[13] Following the 1974 revolution, Belete Gabre Tsadique was called back and appointed to the same post on the strength of his reputation in pre-revolution Ethiopia.

Belete Gabre Tsadique proposed only "moderate" reform measures to the *Derg*, namely tenancy reform, a 1200 hectare ceiling on land ownership, and cadastral survey and registration including land adjudication. The proposed reforms were dismissed out of hand and replaced by a more radical land proclamation known as the "public ownership of rural lands proclamation." Under this proclamation, all land was declared the collective property of Ethiopian people. This draft was prepared by a group of young officials in the Ministry of Land Reform who had secret contact with key members of the *Derg*. While the members of the Cabinet appeared to favor the Minister's proposal, the *Derg* rejected it. The next day, Belete Gabre Tsadique was arrested along with other former senior officials of the Imperial Government. He was freed one year later.

While the issue of agrarian reform was being considered in the 1960s, land grabbing by powerful officials was taking place in the south. For instance, two cabinet ministers each received 280 hectares of forestland under the Emperor's Special Grant Order, only to resell it the following morning. So Aklilu did not have the backing of the Emperor or of the military. However, about the same time that Aklilu was pressing for serious land reform, there was international pressure on the Imperial Government for agrarian change. Among the donor countries that spoke strongly against slow progress in land reform was the Swedish government. Sweden informed the Imperial Government that Swedish assistance in the field of agricultural development might be suspended if Parliament did not enact the draft tenancy proclamation by 1972. The Swedish government's concern was quite understandable given the fact that the Chilalo Agricultural Development Unit (CADU) Project's objective was to uplift the living standards of the small-scale landowners and tenants by raising their productivity. It turned out that the CADU Project's beneficiaries became the main target of eviction by powerful landlords. Eviction of peasants brought about by the combination of green revolution technology and large-scale mechanization became politically controversial among the Swedish politicians, as well as government officials, NGO's, the media and interested citizens.

The United States, one of the major donors, provided a legal advisor to the Ministry of Land Reform and Administration. Secondly, The United States provided overseas training to selected professionals and individuals in order to strengthen the institutional capacity of the new ministry. Other donor agencies, including the World Bank and the European Community also directly or indirectly criticized the Imperial Government for lack of progress in land reform.

In 1971, the Council of Ministers started to deliver on the tenancy reform proposal. The Council was divided between the majority who were opposed to land reform and the minority who felt that it was too late and too little. After a lengthy and heated debate, the bill was approved and presented to Parliament in the autumn of 1972. In May 1973, the chairman announced that Parliament would proceed to vote on the 1971 draft legislation on tenancy. A few days later a final vote was to be taken. However, on the agreed day the chairman refused to let the House proceed to the vote, evidently under personal instruction from the Emperor.[14] As John Cohen rightly stated, "The Emperor and his policy-makers were locked in gradual reform at best, hesitant and piecemeal steps that had not been taken by the time the revolution began."[15]

Ethiopians in the diaspora had expected that during parliamentary recess, the Emperor would use his power to issue legislation by decree, but to the disappointment of millions of his citizens, he blocked passage of an important piece of legislation prior to dissolving the Fourth Parliament. The Emperor of course had always thrown his weight behind landlords, he himself being one of the largest landowners in the country. He also drew his principal domestic support from this group and the Orthodox Church.[16]

While the debate on tenancy reform was going on in Parliament and in high government circles, mass eviction of tenants was taking place on the crown lands in Haikoch and Butagira *Awraja's* (districts) under instruction of the Palace authorities. Only those tenants who were able to pay 150 *birr* (US$72) per 40 hectares were permitted to remain on the land, while the dispossessed tenants were left to squat on unused lands in Sidamo province. Since 150 *birr* is a small amount of money for an Emperor, it is most unlikely that he personally profited from these transactions. It is more likely that officials and other palace dignitaries initiated this scheme in order to enrich themselves using their offices under the authority of the Emperor. The Emperor's position on land reform was often duplicitous. On the one hand, he sought to portray himself as a progressive leader committed to improving the quality of life of his people by making a number of public pronouncements calling for land reform. On the other hand, he was opposed even to modest land reforms. A speech he made in 1961 is illustrative:

> The fundamental obstacle to the full realization of the full measure of Ethiopia's agricultural potential has been, simply stated, lack of security in the land. The fruits of the farmer's labor must be enjoyed by him whose toil has produced the crop. The essence of land reform is, that while respecting the principle of private ownership, that the landless people must have the opportunity to possess their own land, that the position of tenant farmers must be improved, and that the system of taxation applying to land holdings must be the same for all. It is our aim that every Ethiopian should own his own land, in implementation of this principle.[17]

Certainly from his speech, the Emperor appears to show great concern for the plight of small cultivators and tenant farmers, but it is hard to imagine that he would easily change the land tenure system that was the basis of his authority. Haile Selassie's power was greatly increased and inflated as a consequence of the modernization and centralization of the nation-state apparatus. Modernization in Ethiopia had left the land rights system and the role of the State in resource allocation largely unchanged.[18] Haile Selassie used land policies as an instrument to gain political supremacy. The most important method of keeping the loyalty of the military, the aristocracy, and other elite groups was by granting land. To this end, land grants more than doubled after the *coup* of 1960. Of the increase, some 80 percent went to members of the armed forces and the police, whose loyalty was vital to the government.[19] Therefore, the rhetoric was intended only to appease the general public. The following incident is indicative of his true opposition to serious land reform.

In 1969, an international workshop on Agrarian Reform and Rural Development was organized by the Ministry of Land Reform and Administration at the UN ECA's Africa Hall. The workshop was the first of its kind, for it brought together participants from academic institutions, research and training institutes, agricultural extension agencies, government planning offices, and international experts from FAO, USAID, and SIDA to share experience, ideas and information on "agrarian reform" in Ethiopia. It was also the first time in Ethiopian history that land reform was discussed openly and freely. At the conclusion of the conference, but prior to the departure of the international participants, the then Minister of Land Reform and Administration, Fitawrari Abebe Gabre, told this author that he wanted one of the resource persons to brief the Emperor on the outcome of the conference. He added that I should accompany the senior international expert to act as an interpreter, even though the Emperor spoke English. The following day at two p.m. we arrived at the Imperial Palace and were escorted to the Emperor's office. I bowed down in the traditional way and then introduced the expert. The expert briefed the Emperor about the recommendations and conclusions of the conference. As the discussion continued, he also mentioned the similarity between Ethiopia and Iran, and how the Shah of Iran in the 1960s had attempted to bring about land reform in his country. He informed the Emperor that at first the Shah distributed the crown lands to his own tenants. Then, the royal family was told to do the same, and when parliament was out of session, he passed legislation by decree. Tenants were then organized into cooperative societies with access to seasonal credit, marketing, extension, and other governmental services. Before the international expert could complete his point, the Emperor angrily stood up and said, "You mean we have done less for our country than the Shah of Iran?" The expert replied, "Your Majesty, perhaps I have not explained myself well; I apologize for the misunderstanding." Then he began telling the Emperor how great he was, what he had done for

Ethiopia, and how he could make further history by introducing some basic land reform measures in his lifetime. The Emperor demonstrated his anger by walking away from the meeting without even saying goodbye to the renowned international expert who was in his country at the invitation of his own government. The Emperor did not care to listen to what the expert had to say about land reform. His suggestions had proven to be a bitter pill for the Emperor to swallow.[20]

In spite of his modernist pretensions, Haile Selassie was not ready to undermine feudalism completely, nor was he politically strong enough to take significant reform measures. The Emperor's actions were very much influenced by the advice he received from conservative elements in the Senate and the Crown Council, and members of the royal family who were very much opposed to land reform. The brief interaction the expert and this author had with the Emperor made me realize, albeit perhaps too late, that real land reform was going to be very difficult to achieve during the lifetime of the aging Haile Selassie.

4.2 Policies and Priorities in Agriculture

The preceding section examined and analyzed various attempts to bring about land reform in pre-revolution Ethiopia. This section focuses on agricultural strategies, policies, priorities, successes, and failures under the Imperial Government. Agriculture was and is dominant in Ethiopian life. The country is richly endowed with manpower, arable land, and natural resources. However, much of its potential has not yet been realized. Although livestock's contribution to the Ethiopian economy is very limited, the country's livestock resource is the largest in Africa. Historically, the Ethiopian economy has been dominated by peasant agriculture, with the agricultural sector even today contributing over 50 percent of the total GDP, and accounting for about 85 percent of exports and total employment. The country's exports are highly dependent on a single crop, coffee, which generates nearly 60 percent of the foreign exchange earnings. Yet, Ethiopian agriculture has never received the attention, support, and investment commensurate with its contribution to the national economy. The lack of progress in developing agriculture can be attributed to successive Ethiopian governments' general neglect of the sector. As noted in earlier chapters, wrong-headed macro and sector-level policies, traditional feudalistic land tenure systems, the lack of technology development and transfer systems, limited credit and marketing services, inadequate rural infrastructure, as well as periodic droughts, have severely hampered small farmer and therefore overall agricultural sector progress.

In the 1960s, two agricultural production systems existed side by side. The traditional subsistence peasant small-farmer system, and the capitalistic modern commercial large-farmer system. Commercial agriculture in Ethiopia represented a very small percentage, only about five percent, of total agricultural output. The policy of the Imperial Government was to promote the commercialization of the agricultural sector on the basis of private ownership and free market principles.

The Imperial Government allowed agricultural inputs, including farm machinery, chemical fertilizer and pesticides, to be imported duty-free, and in many cases subsidized such imports. The great majority of smaller, poorer farmers could buy few inputs, irrespective of whether they were imported duty-free or subsidized. Therefore, smaller and poorer farmers did not benefit from this policy. Reliable statistics with regard to the number of tractors and other farm machinery that were imported as a result of this new policy are difficult to find. Nevertheless, the lion's share of the country's foreign exchange resources was allocated for this purpose. Imported fuel, machinery, and spare parts were brought into the country at a high cost using scarce foreign exchange. There was no provision for farm tractor and machinery training facilities, and only a handful of technicians were available to do the repair and maintenance work. Therefore, a very high proportion of farm machinery and equipment was simply thrown away for lack of even minor repairs. Furthermore, the large farmers mechanized as they expanded their farming operations, and this resulted in raising rural unemployment. Finally, it should be noted that because mechanization, in order to be cost effective, often called for larger fields, the clearing of boundaries and vegetation led in some cases to serious ecological problems.

Agriculture was not mentioned in the First Five Year Development Plan (1957-62) and the Second Five Year Development Plan (1963-68). Priority was given to infrastructure, manufacturing, mining, and electricity. The Third Five-Year Development Plan (1968-1973) recognized the dual nature of Ethiopia's agriculture and focused on both the modern commercial and traditional peasant agriculture. The plan considered large-scale commercial agriculture as the principal means of boosting agricultural output. This was rationalized as follows:

> The rapid development of commercial agriculture is the only way to get relatively quick increase needed in agricultural exports. It will clearly be essential to induce more foreign private investment and to import the

needed managerial and technical skills; these farming enterprises may be public or private in ownership and operation, but the really important consideration is that the activities be commercially and financially sound. It is from this sector that the rapid gains are expected in output and availability of surpluses, both for consumption domestically, particularly in the cities and towns, as well as for export.[21]

The second strategy was to develop peasant agriculture through area-based programs and by means of a "package of technology." These were government-initiated schemes to promote major agricultural projects in strategically selected areas. The idea was to establish improved agricultural production practices within geographically selected and limited areas. It was envisaged that if the agricultural innovations tried within selected areas were successful, they would be diffused to other areas as well by means of model farmers working under extension agents. Although the "package approach" improved the agricultural productivity of farmers, particularly in the project areas, there were many problems associated with the program. In the Chilalo Agricultural Development Unit (CADU), for instance, the advent of the green revolution technology and mechanization accelerated the large-scale eviction of tenants by powerful landlords. Similarly the CADU Project's success in raising the profit from agricultural production led to increased tenancy rents from one-third to one-half of the harvested crops. Because of the use of improved agricultural technology, especially improved seed, fertilizer and mechanization, large and middle-sized landowners suddenly realized that agriculture could be lucrative. Many commenced to directly engage in farming operations, further complicating the situation for tenants.

One of the qualifications for participation in the credit program was to pay in advance 25 percent of the credit to be provided. In addition, farmers were required to pay cash for fertilizer. It goes without saying that the cash buyers were only the relatively rich. The majority, some 60 percent of the peasants, discontinued buying fertilizer because of their lack of cash. Thus, the credit system favored the big landowners and encouraged tenant eviction.[22]

Smaller farmers and tenants therefore had no inducement to increase production. While they usually continued to grow enough for their own household consumption needs, they had no incentive to produce to meet the demands from the rapidly growing urban and other non-farming population. Farmer participation in decision-making was to be one of the major components of the program. Unfortunately, the projects were conceived, designed, and implemented using a top-down approach in which the project was planned and designed by outside experts in collaboration with staff of the Ministry of Agriculture. There was little or no participation by the local communities. In the case of the CADU Project, involvement by local small farmers was virtually non-existent. The Development Committee, which was the main forum, consisted of representatives of Chilalo's small farmers, local government officials, and CADU staff. The committee held only a few meetings, which were failures in terms of popular participation. The peasants did not dare to voice their problems in front of the government officials and landlords in attendance. So in that sense, real participation did not take place. Effective and genuine participation can take place only if potential beneficiaries are involved through an organization they consider their own.[23]

The Imperial Government's long-term approach to small farmer development was clearly stated in the Third Five-Year Development Plan (1968-1973) as follows:

> Modernization of peasant subsistence agriculture in all areas of the country simultaneously is hardly feasible. It would merely mean dilution of efforts and of limited resources. But no time should be lost in making a start in strategically selected areas in which good results can soon be seen.[24]

The CADU experience made it abundantly clear that, because of the high investment costs, even with external funding, it would not be economically feasible to replicate such projects in other parts of the country. Instead, the Imperial Government, with major donor assistance, decided to focus on a "minimum package approach" as an alternative to area development projects.

In 1971, the government embarked upon the Minimum Package Program (MPP) aimed at the poorer, small farmers, as a lower cost alternative to the large scale and more intensive area development projects like CADU. For each minimum package area, five agricultural extension workers, five marketing assistants, and a supervisor were assigned. Each minimum package area was to support 10,000 peasant families in a given area around a main road so that the necessary infrastructure would be available for transport. The main activities included the demonstration of the effects of using fertilizer in cereal production, the provision of inputs and a credit program to make it possible for the peasants to benefit from the innovations, and cooperative promotion programs.[25]

The aim of the project was to use green revolution technology to increase food production for home consumption and a surplus for the market. It was also intended that each minimum package area would eventually develop into a cooperative society with the help of the marketing advisor. While the idea of providing assistance to the most vulnerable and disadvantaged group of farmers was a step in the right direction, the terms and conditions laid down for this project greatly discouraged small farmer participation in the program. These terms and conditions were:

- Only those who farm on 20 hectares or less could have access to credit.
- Each borrower must have two guarantors.
- Tenants must have a written lease from their landlord, as well as a written permission to participate in the credit program.
- Credit was given in kind, and repayment in cash.
- Interest rate was 12 percent per annum.
- A down payment of 25 percent for fertilizer and 50 percent for seed was required.

By definition these conditions, particularly the down payment, actually prevented most tenants and other peasant farmers from participating as they lacked the necessary cash. The Minimum Package Program thus excluded most of those who would be expected to benefit most from it.[26]

By the mid-1960s, many sectors of the Ethiopian society favored land reform. However, the Emperor's inability to implement meaningful land reform perpetuated a system in which aristocrats and the church owned most of the farmland, and most farmers were tenants who had to provide as much as 50 percent of their crops as rent. As Samuel Huntington once observed,

> Where the conditions of land tenure are equitable and provide a viable living for the peasant, revolution is unlikely. Where they are inequitable and where the peasant lives in poverty and suffering, revolution is likely, if not inevitable, unless the government takes prompt measures to remedy those conditions.[27]

Sad to say, the attitude of the Imperial Government was not to find remedies for the deteriorating socio-economic situation of the country, but to wait and see.

Moreover, in 1973-74, a cruel famine occurred in Wollo province and about 200,000 Ethiopians perished. For months prior to November 1973, the Imperial Government covered up this great unfolding tragedy. It attempted reluctantly to deal with the problem behind the scenes, without international publicity, thus inhibiting rapid delivery of relief supplies from international donors. This triggered the 1974 revolution, which resulted in the demise of the Haile Selassie regime. On September 12, 1974, a creeping putsch that ran over a six-month period culminated in the ascendancy of the military to power.

It would be unfair to close this chapter without mentioning the positive contribution of Haile Selassie to the social and economic development of Ethiopia. Despite his disappointing failure to implement serious land reform measures, and his lack of a quick response to the 1973-74 Wollo famine, Haile Selassie's achievements, particularly in the early years of his reign, were of enormous proportions. He was seen by many as a modernizer, a foresighted monarch, and skillful politician, and above all else a symbol of Ethiopian unity. In the Africa region, he was known as a peacemaker, and spokesperson for African liberation movements. He provided military training, financial, material and moral support to all independent movements on the continent. As a result of his skillful diplomacy, the Organization of African Unity and the United Nations Economic Commission for Africa were established in his capital city, Addis Ababa. When Haile Selassie was finally deposed in 1974, most people in the capital expected and welcomed his downfall, hoping that a better future lie ahead. Sadly, Ethiopia was then devastated for 17 years by terror, war, and starvation under a tyrannical communist regime. After that, over the past nine years, the current regime's ethnic ideology and constitution have negated the oneness and integration of its people, further destroying Ethiopia as a nation.

Sources and Notes

[1] Edmond J. Keller, *Revolutionary Ethiopia: from Empire to People's Republic*, (Indiana University Press, Bloomington and Indianapolis, 1988), p. 61.

[2] Daniel Teffera, *Economic Development and Nation-Building in Ethiopia*, (Ferris State College, Big Rapids, Michigan, 1986), p. 83.

[3] John W. Harbeson, *The Ethiopian Transformation: The Quest for the Post-Imperial State*, (Westview Press, Boulder, Colorado, 1988), p. 33.

[4] Ibid. p 52.

[5] Harold G. Marcus, *A History of Ethiopia*, (University of California Press, Berkeley, Los Angeles and London, 1994), p. 172.

[6] Bahru Zewde, *A History of Modern Ethiopia: 1855-1974*, (Ohio University Press, Athens, Ohio and Addis Ababa University Press, 1991), p. 213.

[7] Harold G. Marcus, op. cit., p. 172.

[8] Edmond J. Keller, op. cit., p. 132.

[9] Patrick Gilkes, *The Dying Lion, Feudalism and Modernization in Ethiopia*, (Julian Friedmann Publishers Ltd, Show Lane, England, UK, 1975), p. 241.

[10] John W. Harbeson, op. cit., p. 52.

[11] Patrick Gilkes, op. cit., p. 101-122.

[12] John Markakis and Nega Ayele, *Class and Revolution in Ethiopia*, (The Red Sea Press, Trenton, New Jersey, 1986), p. 130.

[13] Christopher Clapham, *Transformation and Continuity in Revolutionary Ethiopia*, (Cambridge University, New Rochelle, New York, 1988), p. 33.

[14] Michael Stahl, *Ethiopia: Political Contradictions in Agricultural Development*, (Liber Tryck, Stockholm, 1974), p. 74.

[15] John M. Cohen, *Integrated Rural Development, The Ethiopian Experience and the Debate*, (The Scandinavian Institute of African Studies, Uppsala, Sweden, 1987), p. 41

[16] Michael Stahl, op. cit., p. 167.

[17] Patrick Gilkes, op. cit., p. 70.

[18] Dessaleng Rahmato, "The Ethiopian Experience in Agrarian Reform" in *Challenging Rural Poverty*, edited by Fassil G. Kiros, (Africa World Press, Trenton, New Jersey, 1986), p. 201.

[19] Patrick Gilkes, op. cit., p. 112.

[20] The international expert and authority on agrarian and land reform was Kenneth H. Parsons, a founder of the world-recognized Land Tenure Center at the University of Wisconsin in the USA.

[21] Imperial Government of Ethiopia, *The Third Five-Year Development Plan: 1968-1973*, (Addis Ababa, 1968), p. 191.

[22] Fassil G. Kiros, "Subsistence Crisis in Africa: The Case of Ethiopia," in *Root Causes and Challenges of the 1990s and the New Century*, (Organization for Social Science Research in Eastern Africa, Nairobi, Kenya, 1993), p. 92. Also see Thomas P. Ofcansky and La Verle Berry, *Ethiopia: A Country Study, 4th Edition*, (Federal Research Division, Library of Congress, Government Printing Office, Washington, D.C., 1993), p. 163.

[23] Dharam Ghai, *Participatory Development: Some Perspectives from Grass-Roots Experience*, A paper contributed to the International Conference on Popular Participation in the Recovery and Development Process in Africa, 12-16 February 1990 (Economic Commission for Africa/United Nations, Arusha, United Republic of Tanzania, 1990), p. 3-4.

[24] Imperial Ethiopian Government, op. cit., p. 193.

[25] Michael Stahl, op. cit., p. 107.

[26] Patrick Gilkes, op. cit., p. 125.

[27] Quoted by Howard Handelman, in *The Challenge of THIRD WORLD Development*, (Prentice Hall, Upper Saddle River, New Jersey), p. 113.

Chapter 5

Post-Imperial Development Crises — The *Derg* Era: 1974-1991

In June 1974, the *Derg*, an Amharic word for committee, was established. It had a total of 120 members representing each of the main units of the Army, Air Force, Navy, and the national police. Members of the armed forces had accomplished the revolution. They toppled the ancient regime controlled by an aristocracy and landed oligarchs. The *Derg*, spearheaded by then Major Mengistu Hailemariam, announced the overthrow of Emperor Haile Selassie on September 12, 1974. The *Derg* took the title of Provisional Military Administrative Council (PMAC). It declared socialism to be the guiding ideology of the country, and sponsored the sweeping social and economic reforms described in this chapter.

5.1 Land Reform and Peasant Associations

Sweeping nationalization measures were announced in January and February 1975. Initially banks, other financial institutions, and insurance companies were nationalized. Its first statement on economic policy, "Declaration of Economic Policy of Socialist Ethiopia," was issued in February. Following that statement, a series of radical land reform measures were implemented. The age-old feudal order was overthrown. In March 1975, a new land reform program, "Public Ownership of Rural Land - Proclamation No. 31," was instituted to bring all rural and urban land under government control. The proclamation also included the creation of Peasant Associations that would facilitate implementation of rural development programs and policies. The main provisions of Proclamation No. 31 were:

- All land was the collective property of the Ethiopian people.
- Landlords would receive no compensation for their land.
- Any person willing to cultivate the land would be allotted the use of a plot, up to a maximum of ten hectares for each farm family.

In principle, use of hired labor was prohibited, as was the transfer of land through sale, lease, mortgage, or similar arrangements. Public ownership of land was seen as a solution to the wealth-concentration problem, but the land reform program overlooked the historical significance of private ownership of land in Ethiopia and its impact on incentives to produce. The government ordered all commercial farms to become state farms or remain under state control. The land reform destroyed the feudal order and its system of land tenure; it changed land-ownership and land-use patterns, particularly in the south and southwest in favor of peasants and small landowners. It abolished peasant dependence on the landlord. The majority of the peasantry had access to land. As Legum and Lee put it, "The destruction of the feudal system opened the way for social development in one of the potentially richest countries of Africa."[1] The well-known Africanist, Marina Ottaway, provided a more precise description of the land reform program. She stated, "It would be a mistake to consider the changes in Ethiopia simply a *coup* as a result of which one authoritarian regime has replaced another. The reform has struck a mighty blow against the social base of the landowning class."[2]

The Ethiopian revolution not only succeeded in destroying the feudal structure, but it also promoted equity and equality amongst its citizens. The economic consequences of the land reform were initially some increases in production, mostly due to favorable weather conditions. There was tangible improvement in the peasants' living conditions.[3] However, the urban population suffered because of the sharp price increases that resulted from disruption of the marketing system and an increase in on-farm consumption.[4]

Land reform also provided the opportunity for peasants to be actively involved in local matters by permitting them to form Peasant

Associations of 200-250 farm families each, farming a total area of at least 800 hectares. The government did not possess the administrative capacity to oversee land distribution in the countryside. Instead, it vested a great deal of responsibility in the newly created Peasant Associations to enforce the governments' directives. The peasant beneficiaries were given a strong role in the decision-making process. Having no personnel and little administrative capacity and organization at its disposal to implement the land reform program, the government tried to rely on university and older high school students to provide some leadership and manpower to organize Peasant Associations.[5]

The government recruited more than 60,000 students to go to the rural areas to help mobilize, organize and motivate members of Peasant Associations. In order to lay down the foundation of socialist agriculture, the associations were given the right to establish service cooperatives for marketing, credit, supply, storage, and other services. About ten local Peasant Associations were to be supported by one service cooperative. The Peasant Associations were expected to form producer cooperatives to enable members to work collectively, sharing land and other production inputs. Over time it was intended that the producer cooperatives would become collective farms or agricultural communes. By the end of 1987, there were 20,367 Peasant Associations with a membership of 5.7 million farmers, but not without a high cost in terms of human life and human suffering.

The whole social fabric of Ethiopia was in turmoil. The students tried to introduce changes that were even more radical than those called for by the land reform proclamation. The attempt to establish agricultural communes, such as those in China, created violent confrontation with landlords. In many cases, this set them at odds with the *Derg*. The new regime implemented land reform with the use of widespread coercion and physical violence. Mass mobilization often involved brutal political campaigns asking millions of citizens to rout out and punish alleged enemies of the revolution. Hundreds and thousands were persecuted, jailed, killed, or disappeared. Government attempts to implement land reform also created problems related to security of tenure, which was threatened by increasing pressure from radical elements to quickly distribute land and to collectivize farms. Many peasants were reluctant to improve their land because they were afraid that they would not receive adequate compensation for permanent improvements on their holdings.[6] There was also a general consensus among many farmers that during the land distribution, the fertile, productive land had gone either to rich men who were Peasant

Association officials or to those who could bribe them, or to producer cooperatives.

The Ethiopia land reform effort's shortcomings do not imply that agrarian reform is valueless. Rather it indicates that redistribution of land must take place in a proper political setting and must be supported by additional measures if it is to be effective. For land reform to succeed, the total institutional structure has to be adjusted so that small peasants and farmers gain access to agricultural inputs, education, technical assistance, credit, water, health services, education, irrigation, and other kinds of infrastructure. The objective is to transform traditional peasants and the rural unemployed into efficient producers. Dessalegn Rahmato, in his study of four communities in different parts of Ethiopia, found that as many as 50 per cent of the peasants in some areas did not have oxen and as many as 40 per cent did not have plows.[7] Particularly important are the availability of improved production inputs and the means for their purchase and use by peasants. Otherwise agricultural development will certainly stagnate or decline even after land reform – as it did in Ethiopia.

In 1988, then President Mengistu, who made all significant decisions during the *Derg* era, openly admitted that the country was facing real food shortages as a result of the fall in the rate of growth of agricultural production. He declared:

> It is not difficult to appreciate the impact of the deterioration of production (in agriculture) – the fall in the rate of growth of agricultural production has meant a worsening in the country's food deficit situation. Thus our dependence on the rest of the world with regard to food supply has worsened rather than improved. The negative effect which this dependence has cast on the long history and honor of our country and its people is well recognized. It is hardly necessary to dwell upon the hardship which the declining productivity of agriculture has brought on the country and its people during the past five years.[8]

President Mengistu found the root of the production problem not just in circumstances, but also in social structure. In his view, the heart of the problem was "individualism on the part of the peasant-producer and the old anarchic relationship between the buyer and the seller."[9] The problem became so serious that Mengistu lashed out against the individual and *petit bourgeois* tendencies of the peasantry and their capitalist mentality on the occasion of the fourth anniversary of military rule in September 1978.[10] The Mengistu government's intention was to make the peasant-producer responsible for the dismal performance of agriculture, as had former Soviet Union's leaders blamed the *kulaks*. In

5. President Mengistu Hailemariam

6. The Unpopular "Villagization" Program

fact, over time Mengistu became fully aware that the poor performance of the agricultural sector was the result of his government's commitment to Marxism-Leninism; inadequate infrastructure and the low level of technology; drought and famine which had persisted since the early 1970s; and the ethnic conflict in the north. Some of the major policy failures of the *Derg* regime are discussed below.

5.2 Resettlement

The military government implemented a controversial land settlement policy of moving 1.5 million people from overcrowded and drought-stricken rural areas of the north to relatively less densely populated areas of southern and western Ethiopia by the end of 1985. This plan was far too ambitious when compared to the resources (US$35 million) available for its implementation. The declaration of intent by the government to resettle 1.5 million people unleashed a torrent of controversy. A resettlement program of such magnitude required massive investment in infrastructure, logistics, proper sanitation and health facilities, reasonable housing, and education for settlers.

Another argument surrounding the resettlement program related to the long-term government policy for peasant farms. The long-term objective of the government was to collectivize farms in Ethiopia. The Ten-Year Development Plan had set as its target the collectivization of 50 percent of the farms by 1994. Both bilateral and multilateral donors did not want to support the resettlement program if it was used to recruit labor for Soviet-style collectives and state farms.[11] To move the 1.5 million people scheduled for relocation in 1985, even at the pre-1983 rates, would have cost about 2.1 billion *birr* (US$1 billion). The entire Ethiopian budget was only 2.9 billion *birr* (US$1.4 billion) in 1982.[12] These figures do not include transportation, perhaps the most costly item of all.

The government was also criticized for its gross human rights violations, forced separation of families, and lack of medical attention in resettlement centers that resulted in thousands of deaths from malaria and sleeping sickness. An estimated 50,000 to 100,000 of those resettled in this massive program had died by July 1985 as a result of disease brought about by wretched conditions in the resettlement areas.[13]

Critics within the international community charged that the military government's resettlement program served as an obstacle to dealing more effectively with the problems of drought and famine relief. The government on the other hand claimed that it was carrying out the program for humanitarian reasons, contending that it would move the people from the exhausted and unproductive land and settle them in areas with rich agricultural potential. This policy of large-scale population resettlement schemes first began under Haile Selassie, during the major drought in 1973, as a means of reducing population congestion in the north and developing virgin lands in the south and southwest. But the large-scale resettlement schemes were continued and intensified by the Mengistu regime supposedly to alleviate soil erosion, over-population and destructive farm practices. Many people outside Ethiopia claimed that the *Derg* regime used resettlement as an anti-insurgency tool in Tigray. However, those who spread such malicious stories were labeled opponents of the regime and its ideology.

As a World Food Program official (1977-1980), one of the author's responsibilities was monitoring WFP inputs to insure that the food aid was appropriately distributed to resettlement schemes, including the resettlement district at Assosa, 300 miles west of Addis Ababa. The majority of the settlers were from Wollo, Gondar, and Shoa. It is the author's conclusion that the government's action was based on humanitarian and economic considerations alone. Although the original target was to move a million and half people to new resettlement areas, when the campaign came to an end in February 1986, the actual number was about 600,000.[14] The program was halted as a result of pressure on the military government from international donors and agencies.

5.3 Villagization

In 1985, the government initiated a new relocation program known as villagization. Under the program, farmers were forced to combine their lands and live in communal villages. The stated official goal of the program, which grouped scattered farming communities throughout the country into small vi lage clusters, was to improve the access of rural residents to social services and to strengthen the abilities of rural communities to defend themselves. Another motive, however, appeared to be the conversion of villagized communities into producer cooperatives or collectives, as well as into centers for military recruitment. As Christopher Clapham wrote:

One function of villagization, even short of using it to induce the formation of producers' cooperatives, is to make it very much easier for the Agricultural Marketing Corporation to extract produce from peasants at controlled prices, and correspondingly more difficult for peasants to earn higher incomes by evading the official market.[15]

Edmond Keller also maintained that the long-term goal of the program was to convert villagized communities into producer cooperatives.[16]

Following the war between Ethiopia and Somalia in 1977, the security situation in the south and southeast rapidly deteriorated. In order to protect the security of widely dispersed farmers it was essential to bring them together in villages. By 1989, the government had already villagized about 13 million peasants in more than 4,500 villages in Shoa, Arsi and Hararge provinces in order to strengthen self-defense, as well as for the reasons mentioned above. As time passed, the *Derg* faced growing opposition from every quarter. There was strong condemnation from international donors and agencies, as well as lack of resources. Like resettlement, villagization generally caused a good deal of social disruption. Families usually were required to move from their traditional location, close to their customary farming plots into clustered villages where the land to be cultivated often was on fragmented plots far from the homestead.

In 1986 the Swedish International Development Agency (SIDA) commissioned a valuable study of the impact of the villagization program. The report of the two-person mission pointed out that the 1985-1986 initiative was poorly timed and should not be continued until an evaluation of the first phase of project activities was accomplished. Furthermore, the report recommended that further villagization be postponed until certain technical, environmental, and marketing problems were addressed and solved, or at least until the first phase of the program had been adequately evaluated.[17] International criticism, deteriorating security conditions, and lack of resources doomed the plan to failure. In 1990, the government essentially abandoned villagization when it announced new free-market economic policies.

5.4 State Farms

The state farms are far more straightforward organizations than are collective farms.[18] They are simply large-scale nationalized farms that are owned and managed directly by the state and the people who work on them are employees receiving a wage or salary for their work. State farms are primarily designed to demonstrate the advantage of largeness of scale in agriculture, and in this way play a part in encouraging the peasants to form the collectives. State farms are supposed to be largely responsible for improving technology. Examples are the production of improved seed and high quality livestock, and the testing of new technologies not previously used under farm conditions.

Prior to the revolution of 1974, there already were a small number of small private farms developed either as settlement schemes or as schemes to attract foreign capital. Also there were a small number of larger private farms that produced commercial crops using modern agricultural technology. These two types of farms were combined to constitute the state sector in agriculture after 1975. State farms increased from 72,000 hectares at the time of the 1975 land reform to 232,000 hectares in 1982. State farm grain production increased from 1.5 million quintal before the revolution to 4.5 million quintal in 1988.

The establishment of state farms shortly after the start of the revolution and their rapid expansion stemmed from the military government's belief that this was the best way to provide a reliable marketable surplus of food grains for the urban population and the army. But state farms had a number of economic management and financial difficulties. Between 1978/79 and 1982/83, for example, between 58 percent and 64 percent of government resources spent in agriculture were devoted to the state farms, with much of the remainder also going to other large-scale schemes.

As shown in Table 6, in 1982/83, the state farms, with just over four percent of the cultivated area, received 76 percent of the total allocation of chemical fertilizer, 96 percent of the improved seeds, and 81 percent of agricultural credit. In terms of subsidies, between 1982/83 and 1985/86 the various state farm corporations received more than 90 million *birr* (US$434,000) in direct subsidies. Despite the emphasis on state farms, state farm production accounted for only six percent of total agricultural output in 1987, leaving peasant farmers responsible for 90 percent of production.[19]

TABLE 6
FERTILIZER, SEED, AND CREDIT DISTRIBUTION: 1982/1983
(% of total)

	Chemical Fertilizer	*Improved Seed*	*Agricultural Credit*
Peasants/ Cooperatives	23.6	4.1	12.3
State Farms	76.4	95.8	80.9
Settlements	----	1.1	6.8

Source: Agricultural Marketing Corporation (1982), and Ethiopian Seed Corporation (1984).

But the benefits from such productivity were achieved at a financial cost that can only be justified on ideological grounds. Most state farms were operating in the red with total recorded losses in 1986/87 of 65 million *birr* (US$31 million). In 1988/89 losses mounted to 115 million *birr* (US$55 million). The emphasis on mechanization required major investment of scarce foreign exchange resources. Therefore, other development needs requiring foreign exchange were constrained. Mengistu himself accurately described the actual failure of state farms:

> While the yield of state farms should be an average of 25 quintals of wheat per hectare, the results so far achieved do not exceed a yield of 14 quintal per hectare, and this is not much superior to the amount produced in many areas by peasants using backward implements. Even the maize crop produced by the state farms is hardly higher then that produced by peasants in terms of yield per hectare. It is clearly recognizable that the lack of detailed studies of the sites of certain state farms has contributed to their operational inefficiency, low productivity, and diminishing sizes. The fundamental reason, however, remains to be the inherent defect in the utilization of manpower and equipment, and, as a whole, lack of control over the widespread inefficiency of management.[20]

5.5 Agricultural Producer Cooperatives

In centrally planned economies such as the former Soviet Union and China, the establishment of cooperatives was merely a step on the way to complete collectivization of agriculture. Since the Soviet experience was a prototype for the Ethiopian revolution, the military leaders in

Ethiopia believed in the creation of a collectivized industrial agricultural system by which economies of scale could be achieved through massive infusions of capital goods and large-scale production. There was a strong belief that small farmers were inefficient and were unable to take advantage of economies of scale.

As a consequence, the government ordered the creation of cooperatives. The collectivization strategy was considered to be the cornerstone of the Ethiopian revolution, although it eventually turned out to be a failure. The 1979 proclamation on producer cooperatives clearly stated that peasants should voluntarily join producer cooperatives. The proclamation made it clear that force or coercion was not to be applied. Yet, the military government provided a number of inducements to producer cooperatives, including priority for credit, fertilizer, improved seed, and access to consumer items and building materials and the sale of such items at a reduced price.[21]

The idea was to collectivize the agricultural sector step by step starting with voluntary cooperatives in the early stages of the revolution. Yet, the cooperatives performed no better than peasant farms in terms of production; nor were they able to improve the living standards of their members to any significant extent. Hence, there was no real incentive for the peasants to opt for cooperative farming in preference to family farming. In other words, even with the incentives, farmers responded less than enthusiastically. They saw the move to form cooperatives as a prelude to the destruction of their family farms. By 1985/86 there were only 2,323 producer cooperatives, of which only 255 were registered.

TABLE 7
ESTIMATE OF YIELDS AFTER LAND REFORM

Farm Type	Total Cropland (%)	Total Production (%)	Quintal/Hectare
Peasant	87	96	13
Group	3	2	10
State	2	2	17

Sources: CSO Agricultural Sample Survey, 1979/80, Volume 11, Area, Production, and Yield of Major Crops, (Addis Ababa, Ethiopia, May 1980).

As shown above, 13 quintals per hectare was the average yield on peasant farms, while yields on state farms was 17 quintals per hectare. The average yield on state farms was not that much greater than on peasant farms. Producer cooperatives yielded only 10 quintals per hectare, an amount much lower than the yield from either the private peasant holdings or the state farms. This is surprising considering that many cooperatives had attempted to mechanize, and made themselves dependent on imported fuel, machinery, and spare parts. Both group and state farms were large-scale enterprises that had access to production technologies, and were given more attention and encouragement by the military government than peasant farms. However, they produced only a small percentage of total production. By far the greater percentage of land was under smallholder cultivation, which also supplied almost all of the agricultural produce of the country. Notwithstanding the poor performance of collective agriculture, the Mengistu regime continued to give emphasis to collectivization for economic and political reasons. Reasons given were that the peasant class represented a capitalist or latent capitalist element that was ideologically unacceptable, and it was more efficient to control the peasantry on large farms than in smaller units. Moreover, by forcing peasants into large collectives, agricultural prices and wages could be controlled at low levels to allow capital to accumulate for industrial expansion; and strict control would facilitate the flow of foodstuffs to the cities in order to feed the growing industrial activities.[22] These policies and strategies were influenced by alien doctrines, which failed to examine the nature and characteristics of the Ethiopian "problem."

When the military junta took power in 1974, Haile Selassie's government was accused of neglect and cover up of the "Wollo" famine. Exactly ten years after the Imperial Government had been discredited and over thrown, Ethiopia faced one of the worst droughts in memory. Mengistu was informed about the impending danger, but pretended as if nothing were happening. He wanted nothing to interfere with the ten-year anniversary of the military coming to power and creation of the Workers Party of Ethiopia (WPE). It was during this period that the program and charter of the WPE was approved. The Workers Party Congress also adopted the basic directives for the Socio-Economic Development of Ethiopia (1984/85-1993/94). While Mengistu was busy entertaining his foreign visitors and dignitaries, mostly from the communist-block countries, with lavish and most expensive parties, the question of hunger and famine was not mentioned even once. Instead he talked about the glory and achievements of the Ethiopian revolution. A huge amount of money – David Korn estimates between US$50 to 100 million – was spent on the celebrations that included the beautification of Addis Ababa, erection of numerous monuments, and a new Party Congress Hall.[23]

While spending millions to build Soviet-style state farms and collectives, Mengistu covered up the magnitude of the famine by refusing to allow Western news media to visit the drought areas until after the tenth anniversary of the revolution had been celebrated. Meanwhile thousands of Ethiopians were dying in Wollo and Tigray. By early 1985, some 7.7 million people were suffering from drought and famine. Of that number, 2.5 million were at immediate risk of starving. More than 300,000 died in 1984 alone, more than twice the number that died in the drought a decade before. A major famine also occurred in 1987-88, but massive efforts mounted by international donors prevented another major catastrophe. By the end of the decade, one million Ethiopians had died from drought and famine.[24]

As if Ethiopia did not have enough problems, the military junta introduced "compulsory delivery at fixed prices" for agricultural crops. Artificially low prices for agricultural produce were enforced and farmers were not allowed to sell their surplus produce on the open market. Government statements stressed that the deliveries were "of the nature of a tax" and there were penalties for non-fulfillment. Reducing the incentives to grow food led to reduced food production; the result was higher food prices and waves of discontent in urban centers.

In the socialist countries of Eastern Europe, there was a system of "compulsory deliveries at fixed prices." It was initially introduced after the 1917 Bolshevik revolution. The process of taking capital from agriculture for the establishment and expansion of a developing economy comes within what Marx called "primitive accumulation" – as distinct from the "accumulation of capital" wherein manufacturers put aside some of their own surplus capital from production for further investment.[25] The economy of Ethiopia is overwhelmingly rural in nature, and the military government sought to industrialize it. It is hardly surprising, therefore, that the regime attempted to extract resources from agriculture and channel them into manufacturing and industry. Many nations seeking to industrialize have done this.

Farmers were told what to grow and they had to sell their crops to the government at (low) fixed prices. By imposing price controls on food crops, Mengistu's government further impoverished its farm population and created disincentives for food production. Anxious to assure a supply of cheap food for its more influential urban population, the government controlled prices of basic commodities, thus pushing prices below their free-market value. Unsurprisingly, crop harvests remained very low.

The USAID Deputy Administrator properly stated,

> In Ethiopia the problem is fundamental. They are taking a bad
> ecological situation and making it worse. By forcing farmers who do
> grow more than they consume to sell to the state at prices below the cost
> of production, they are not providing the incentives to produce the
> maximum that the land however poor would yield.[26]

The World Bank, the European Community, and the USAID all
advocated incentive programs for agriculture and industry, more free
trade within the country, as well as more imports. The World Bank
alone, then Ethiopia's largest source of donor funds, would have
doubled its highly concessional loan program (which totaled US$403
million between 1980 and 1984) if Ethiopia would implement some of
the suggested economic reforms. The European Community and the
World Bank withheld US$250 million in development aid for Ethiopia
until the Mengistu government would agree to raise artificially low
prices for agricultural products and allow farmers to sell more of their
products on the open market.[27]

However, the Mengistu regime was not willing to listen, even to
such powerful donors as the World Bank. One U.S. Republican
Congressman introduced a bill in Congress for severe economic
sanctions against Ethiopia. Similarly, a Texas Democrat and chairman
of the Select Committee on Hunger criticized the Ethiopian
government. He recommended a ban on aid, but continued
humanitarian assistance. As Magistad rightly pointed out, the country
that was perhaps the most desperately in need of development
assistance in the world received the least aid of any country in Africa.[28]
Aid per capita in 1989 was US$14. According to one calculation,
Ethiopia was receiving only US$6 per head in official development
assistance compared to about US$18 for sub-Saharan Africa as a whole
in 1982.[29]

In March 1990, the authoritarian Mengistu Hailemariam proposed
scrapping Ethiopia's rigid Soviet-style economic system and its
replacement by a mixed economy with a free market. In an hour-long
speech to the Central Committee of the ruling Marxist Worker's Party,
Mengistu turned his back on more than 15 years of central state
planning and conceded it had been a failure.[30] In addition, Mengistu,
and his party took a number of small, half-hearted steps to attract
foreign investment and encourage domestic production by allowing
developers to build houses, apartment housing, and office buildings for
rent or sale. At that time, the government held all land and commercial
property deeds. He also allowed the sale or closure of government's

myriad of state-owned industries and business enterprises that continued to lose money, and to retain those that were profitable. Among the specific reforms Mengistu introduced were:

- Allowing the private sector to take part in all sectors of the economy with no limit on capital investment. Ethiopia had had a US$250,000 ceiling on all types of private investment.
- Giving government land on a concessional basis to private commercial firms for construction of industries, hotels, etc.
- Free movement of goods, market deregulation, providing farmers with security of tenure.
- Allowing a greater role for private capital in efforts to stimulate a stagnant economy, including private investment in agriculture for the first time since the 1974 revolution.[31]

Mengistu's 1990 decision to introduce free-market economic reforms was designed to reverse the decline in Ethiopia's agricultural sector. There were many debates as to whether or not these reforms were genuine and how effectively they could be implemented. Nonetheless, agricultural output rose by an estimated three percent in 1990/91, almost certainly in response to the relaxation of government regulations. This modest increase, however, was not enough to offset a general decrease in GDP during the same period. The *Derg* era ended abruptly in May 1991.

Sources and Notes

[1] C. Legum and B. Lee, *Conflict in the Horn of Africa*, (African Studies Association Press, New York, 1977), p. 20.

[2] Marina Ottaway, "Socialist Classes and Corporate Interest in the Ethiopian Revolution," in *Journal of Modern African Studies, Volume 14*, (Cambridge University Press, 1976), p. 469-80.

[3]. Marina Ottaway, "Land Reform in Ethiopia, 1974-1977" in *African Studies Review, Volume 20*, (African Studies Review Association, East Lansing, Michigan, 1977), p. 79-90.

[4] Ibid., p. 85

[5] Thomas P. Ofcansky and LaVerle Berry, Editors, *Ethiopia: A Country Study*, 4th Edition, (Federal Research Division, Library of Congress, US Government Printing Office Washington, D.C., 1993), p. 170.

[6] Mulatu Wubneh and Yohannis Abate, *Ethiopia: Transition and Development in the Horn of Africa*, (Westview Press, Boulder, Colorado, 1988), p. 95.

[7] Dessaleng Rahmato, "The Ethiopian Experience in Agrarian Reform" in *Challenging Rural Poverty*, edited by Fassil G. Kiros, (Africa World Press, Trenton, New Jersey, 1986), p. 150.

[8] Fassil G. Kiros, *The Subsistence Crisis in Africa: The Case of Ethiopia – Root Causes and Challenges of the 1990s and the New Century*, (Organization for Social Science Research in Eastern Africa, Nairobi, Kenya, 1993), p. 150.

[9] John W. Harbeson, *The Ethiopian Transformation: The Quest for the Post-Imperial State*, (Westview Press, Boulder, Colorado, 1988), p. 172.

[10] Thomas P. Ofcansky and LaVerle Berry, op. cit., p. 173.

[11] Mulatu Wubneh and Yohannis Abate, op. cit., p. 101.

[12] Reported in October 1, 1985 *Wall Street Journal* article by Robert Kaplan and cited in *Politics and the Ethiopian Famine*, Jason W. Clay and Bonnie K. Holcomb, *1984-1985*, (The Red Sea Press, Trenton, New Jersey, 1986), p. 99.

[13] Christopher Clapham, *Transformation and Continuity in Revolutionary Ethiopia*, (Cambridge University, New Rochelle, New York, 1988), p. 193.

[14] Edmond J. Keller, *Revolutionary Ethiopia: from Empire to People's Republic*, (Indiana University Press, Bloomington and Indianapolis, Indiana, 1988), p. 229.

[15] Christopher Clapham, op. cit., p. 178.

[16] Edmond J. Keller, op. cit., p. 228.

[17] John M. Cohen and Nils-Ivar Isaksson, *Villagization in the Arsi Region of Ethiopia*, Report prepared by SIDA Consultants to the Ethio-Swedish Mission on Villagization in the Arsi Region, December 1-14, 1986, Rural Development Studies No. 19, (Swedish University of Agricultural Sciences, International Rural Development Centre, Uppsala, February 1987).

[18] The Russian *soukhozi* was the model for Ethiopia's state farms during the *Derg* era.

[19] Ajit Kumar Ghose, "Transforming Feudal Agriculture: Agrarian Change in Ethiopia since 1974," in *The Journal of Development Studies, Volume 22, No. 1*, (Frank Cass & Co., Ltd. London, October 1985), p. 134.

[20] Christopher Clapham, op. cit., p. 181.

[21] Alemneh Dejene, *Peasants, Agrarian Socialism, and Rural Development in Ethiopia*, (Westview Press, Boulder and London, 1987) p. 74.

[22] David L. Clawson and James S. Fisher, *World Regional Geography: A Development Approach, 6th Edition*, (Prentice Hall, Upper Saddle River, New Jersey, 1992), p. 283.

[23] See Jason W. Clay and Bonnie K. Holcomb, op. cit., p. 216.

[24] Michael S. Serill, "Why are the Ethiopians Starving Again? What should the world do and not do?" *Time Magazine*, (Time-Life Inc., New York, December, 21, 1989), p. 22-27.

[25] Jack Duman, *Agriculture: Capitalist, Socialist*, (Cambridge University Press, Cambridge, UK, 1988), p. 201.

[26] Mary Kay Magistad, "When the shouting stops: Ethiopian Relief Revisited", *Development International*, (Development International, Washington, D.C., July/August 1987), p. 34.

[27] Michael S. Serill, op. cit., p. 22-27.

[28] Mary Kay Magistad, op. cit., p. 34.

[29] United Nations, *African Recovery: Country Profiles, Volume 5, Numbers 2-3*, (United Nations, Department of Public Information, September 1991), p. 28.

[30] Article entitled, "Mengistu Ditches Marxist Policies," *Daily Nation of Kenya*, (Daily Nation of Kenya, Nairobi, March 6, 1990).

[31] Ibid.

Chapter 6

Post-*Derg* Development Crises – The EPRDF Era: 1991-1999

After having brought Ethiopia to ruin, dictator Mengistu Hailemariam fled the country in May 1991. One week later, the Ethiopian Peoples Revolutionary Democratic Front (EPRDF) marched into Addis Ababa and assumed power. Diaspora Ethiopians were full of optimism that there would be political stability, multi-party democracy and pluralism, a free market economy, property rights, and the rule of law in their native country. Many also had hoped that the wars that ravaged the country for decades would be a thing of the past once changes in the political order took place. They were confident that a time of reconciliation, peace, reconstruction, and freedom had arrived. A large number of patriotic Ethiopians were eager to return to their country to invest and participate in nation-building after spending many years abroad.

In July 1991, the EPRDF convened a national conference of some 24 ethnic political groups under the umbrella of the EPRDF.[1] Regretfully, the meeting excluded representatives of the large independent opposition political parties. These parties were the Southern Ethiopian Peoples' Coalition (SEPDC), the All Amhara Peoples Organization (AAPO), the Coalition of Ethiopian Democratic Forces (COEDF), the Council of Alternative Forces for Peace and Democracy in Ethiopia (CAFPDE), the Afar Revolutionary Democratic Unity Party (ARDUP), the Ethiopian Medhin Democratic party

(MEDHIN) and a few others. Their membership comprised some 80 percent of the total Ethiopian population.

The purpose of the EPRDF conference was to set up a transitional government, and draw up a charter that would become the supreme law of the country. Observers wonder how it could become the supreme law of the country when the parties that represented most Ethiopians were not allowed to participate in the conference. Under the umbrella of the EPRDF, all power was held by the Tigrean People's Liberation Front (TPLF) with the charismatic leadership of its chairman, Meles Zenawi.[2] Other parties were forbidden or subsumed under the TPLF. Thus, Ethiopia became virtually a one-party state while giving the impression to the outside world that it had become a multi-party state.

7. Prime Minister Meles Zenawi

When the Transitional Government of Ethiopia (TGE) was established, the TPLF and members of its satellite ethnic parties held virtually all positions of political and economic influence. The Amhara ethnic group, the second largest ethnic group with some 30 percent of Ethiopia's total population, was denied political and economic power. No senior positions in the transitional government were assigned to persons from the Amhara ethnic group. Observers had expected power-sharing arrangements that would seek to create ethnic tranquillity and stability by constitutionally dividing political control among major ethnic groups.

In addition to the national conference of 1991, local and regional elections took place in 1992. There has been intense debate concerning the extent to which the TPLF, initially via the EPRDF-controlled TGE and later via the Federal Democratic Republic of Ethiopia (FDRE), is committed to democratic governance. The record is clear that it has fallen short of the norms and principles that it continues to profess. According to Donald Crummey, the EPRDF has little or no commitment to democratization, and its espousal of this cause is simply a gesture to those governments and NGO's whose favor it now seeks. This suspicion is fueled by the TPLF's longstanding commitment to Marxist-Leninist ideology.[3]

In an attempt to maintain absolute control over the University of Addis Ababa, the government summarily dismissed the university president, two vice-presidents and thirty-nine other faculty in early 1993. Most of those dismissed and imprisoned were of the previously influential Amhara ethnic group. This was a crushing blow to a human capital-poor country like Ethiopia with its critical shortage of trained manpower. During the TGE period, both the Council of Representatives and the executive branch took measures beyond the conventional power limits of a provisional government. The internal and international boundaries of the country were redrawn, the state bureaucracy was dismantled, and about 80,000 government personnel were dismissed in the name of structural adjustment. They were frequently replaced by poorly qualified TPLF/EPRDF loyalists. Furthermore, Tigrayan persons acquired most of the privatized government parastatal firms.

What was perhaps more surprising and shocking to Ethiopians was the division of their country's territory along ethnic lines even while apartheid was being dismantled in South Africa. Observers could hardly believe Ethiopians would be forcibly segregated into ethnic states or *killils* as in former South Africa. The setting up of ethnic *killils* followed the pattern of *Bantustanization* established to enforce apartheid in South Africa.[4]

6.1 Economic Policies

During the nearly two decades of *Derg* government, Ethiopia's economic performance was constrained by overall economic structural problems resulting from Marxist and otherwise wrong-headed economic policies being implemented by the *Derg* regime. Since 1990, Ethiopia has gradually scrapped those failed policies, including central planning, in favor of a market economy. It is pursuing a more capitalistic path of development that emphasizes increasing production by attracting foreign investment and providing incentives to local entrepreneurs.

In November 1991, the Transitional Government issued a new economic policy statement that laid the cornerstone for improving the overall policy environment. With support of the International Monetary Fund and the World Bank, its goals were to deregulate the country's economy, privatize public enterprises, encourage the promotion of domestic and foreign private investment, devalue its currency, and implement structural adjustment programs. Furthermore, with the abolition of the compulsory quota delivery system at pre-set prices, agricultural prices were virtually deregulated. Farmers could grow what they wanted to grow, and sell to anyone at whatever price they could get. The transfer of resources through the artificially created, unfavorable internal terms of trade for agriculture was greatly minimized. Thus the policy of maintaining "cheap food and agricultural commodities" to benefit the urban centers and non-farm sectors was almost wholly discontinued. Producer cooperatives and collectives were mostly dissolved, smallholder and private commercial farms were encouraged, public investment in state farms was drastically reduced and an open market for grain sales was restored.[5]

A new long-term economic development strategy was adopted in August 1992, entitled the Agricultural Development-led Industrialization (ADLI) strategy. It stated that agricultural development is the springboard for the country's overall development.[6] The EPRDF government policies have, in general, been much more oriented to the rural areas than those of the *Derg* regime. None-the-less, even with its achievements in the rural and agricultural sectors, there are still major unresolved institutional and structural issues. These include land policies, annexation of new lands, and ethnic regionalism. All of these hamper the economic development of the country.

6.2 Land Policies

One bias against agriculture that has continued under the present regime is the issue of land tenure. Simply put, private urban property such as business enterprises can be sold or mortgaged even under the present government's urban land-lease system. By contrast, there are no such rights for peasant-operated farm plots. This policy incongruity confers a higher degree of property ownership on urban business enterprises than on rural agricultural activities, with considerable consequences on the overall incentive system.

The EPRDF government essentially adopted the previous regime's land policies so farmers are not allowed to buy and sell land. They can inherit the right only to work a piece of land or lease it. A successful farmer cannot buy to expand his farm or use it for collateral to obtain credit. The government fears that in a bad year small farmers would sell their land and drift into towns where there is no work. A second assertion is that peasant farmers are afraid of being expropriated by former landowners. These political arguments may be convincing on the surface, but are actually little more than political rhetoric.

The disastrous economic consequences of state ownership of land under the *Derg* regime are well documented. Collective ownership of farmland gave rise to indifference to maintaining the quality and sustainability of productive soil. Ethiopian farmers do not have the incentives under collective usufruct rights to conserve the environment. This has resulted in accelerated deforestation over the past two and a half decades. Similarly, state ownership of land has adversely affected security of tenure, and therefore investment in agriculture, adoption of new technology and potential productivity.

It has been proven time and again around the world that state ownership and control of farmland results in failure. In several countries, e.g., the Baltic states and Ukraine, peasants now have the right to own and lease land and farm independently. In 1993, President Boris Yeltsin signed a decree that made it legal for the first time since 1917 for Russians to own land. With the collapse of Eastern European communism and the development of "market socialism" in China and Vietnam, the failures of command economies have become more evident. China, which during the 1950s and 1960s implemented one of the world's most extensive collectivized farm programs, subsequently reversed direction dramatically. With the introduction of its "responsibility system" in 1980, China's communist government returned collective farmland to family plots. From 1980 to 1984, the value of agricultural output rose approximately 40 percent.[7]

Sisay Asefa was dead right when he said:

> The collapse of the former USSR and the communist economic system has to do, for the most part, with the denial of property and land rights by government to citizens. In fact, a country cannot really have a market economy if a major factor of production such as land is owned by the state.[8]

The economic policy adopted by the EPRDF government in 1992 on "land ownership" appears to be guided primarily by the narrow objective of the government to control the nation's wealth and thereby to tighten its grip on the Ethiopian people. For example, the "agrarian reform" program in Region 3 (Amhara), implemented in 1997, clearly shows how the EPRDF government uses land as a weapon to punish its enemies and reward its supporters.

About 1300 farmers from Gojjam were dispossessed of their land. That land was redistributed to supporters of the ruling party. Local officials were deliberately abusive and demoralizing in responding to the farmers' complaints. Angry peasants traveled to Addis Ababa to protest against their land being confiscated by the regional authorities. The central government told the farmers that decisions regarding land redistribution should be made at the regional level and to return to Gojjam immediately.

It was decided later by the Region 3 government that landowners during the reign of Haile Selassie or the military junta era could not own more than one hectare of land, while peasants who were oppressed by those former regimes were entitled to three hectares. Economic considerations such as family size, ability of the farm family to farm, and fertility of the land were not considered. The effect of this policy was to expropriate land from farmers with landholdings not exceeding ten hectares in order to benefit poor peasants whom the EPRDF was trying to attract as supporters.[9] The army's brutal treatment of the peasants was so widespread that it nearly brought direct confrontation with local authorities. This kind of isolated and dangerous confrontation with local officials is likely to spread unless the government shows moderation in its treatment of the farmers and equitable distribution of resources.

The issues related to land ownership can be argued endlessly. As Mamo Muchie opines, "The debate on whether or not private or collective property ownership is appropriate should be judged on the qualitative improvement it brings to peasants' well being, learning, functioning and capabilities."[10] There is nothing more important to

Ethiopians than land and the issue of ownership should be presented for referendum to the Ethiopian people. The question of ownership should not be a matter for urban elites to decide in their safe comfort far away from the realities of peasant life. The author agrees with Mamo Muchie that ownership should be decided with the full involvement of the peasant beneficiaries themselves.

There are major economic policy biases against agriculture still prevalent in Ethiopia. However, these are not necessarily the most important constraints to the development of agriculture. More fundamental policy stances, some outside the realm of economics, may play a much more decisive role in shaping the fate of agriculture in Ethiopia. These include the degree of democratization in the political system, existence of the rule of law, basic human rights of expression and association, as well as property ownership.

The author believes that the Ethiopian government's main tasks should be the maintenance of law and order, development of physical and human infrastructure, environmental protection, promotion of improved agricultural technology and its use by farmers, and the defense of the country. For example, it would be the task of the state, with input from affected citizens, to say whether a particular road were needed at all, to choose the route, to set the rules for contracts for construction, and oversee construction, as well as the road's maintenance. Ronald Hope Kempe argues, "Economic progress blossoms best when economic freedom, expressed through the market place, is promoted and enhanced – state intervention is now equated with economic retardation and has consequently become a discredited framework."[11]

6.3 Annexation of New Lands

Another issue is the incorporation of fertile territory from other regions, namely Gondar and Wollo, into Region 1 (Tigray) to fulfill the TPLF dream of a "Greater Tigray" – without a mandate to do so from the Ethiopian people. In 1992, seven districts from northern Gondar and Wollo that are inhabited by the Amhara ethnic group were forcibly added to Region 1. Prior to this annexation, the populations of Wollo and Gondar were not consulted, nor was the Ethiopian nation. There is no historical or other basis for this action, except that these districts are the most fertile lands in the region. It is well known that most of Tigray is resource-depleted as the land has been exploited for centuries. This *killil* could not become self-sufficient in food at least in the immediate future. Therefore, the government chose to annex the land that was traditionally the home of other ethnic groups by force of arms. The TPLF's major concern appears to be the consolidation of its power base by developing economic resources that will enable it to withstand any attempts from outside Tigray to adversely affect its goal of having the potential to be economically self-sufficient.

To this end, the government was very active in developing the necessary infrastructure and resettling Tigrayan returnees from Sudan and demobilized TPLF soldiers in these districts. By resettling Tigrayan returnees and demobilized TPLF soldiers among the Amhara ethnic population, the TPLF tried to change the ethnic configuration of the annexed area with a view to ensuring that the majority of the settlers are from Tigray. To reinforce its plan, the language of instruction in the government primary schools quickly changed from Amharic to Tigregna, even though a substantial number of Amhara families still remained in the districts. As time passed, the TPLF evicted the peasants of Northern Gondar and Wollo from their ancestral lands and annexed these areas to Tigray. The ethnically cleansed peasants from these places are now landless paupers; many exploited as cheap farm labor by the expropriators of their land. Others are forced to survive as beggars in Gondar, Dessie, and Bahar Dar.[12]

Table 8 indicates the ethnic composition and mother tongue of the seven districts in Gondar and Wollo.

TABLE 8
ETHNIC COMPOSITION AND MOTHER TONGUE IN SEVEN
DISTRICTS: WOLLO AND GONDAR REGIONS (1991)

District	Ethnic Composition		Mother Tongue	
	Amhara	Tigraway	Amharic	Tigregna
Gondar				
Humera	3,780	41,999	3,771	43,510
Tselemt	10,382	87,012	12,428	85,114
Welkait	2,734	87,099	2,482	87,610
Tsegede	14,226	45,532	16,082	43,719
Totals	31,122	261,642	34,763	259,953
Wollo				
Raya Azebo	8,466	76,431	9,679	74,951
Alamata	31,761	58,244	34,164	57,467
Ofla	4,304	11,038	6,149	109,632
Totals	51,265	145,713	49,992	242,050

Source: Ethiopian Register, September 1996.

This action by the provisional government has been condemned by the entire population of Ethiopia and especially by the Amhara ethnic group. Instead of introducing a legal system that protects equality, provides justice to all linguistic and ethnic groups, and is committed to fostering the conditions that reduce hunger and increase the welfare of its citizens, the EPRDF government has chosen to launch an ethnic vendetta that creates confusion and turmoil. The Ethiopian people must be allowed to determine their future not through the barrel of the gun but through the ballot box.

Considering the gravity of this situation and its future implications, two prominent Ethiopians from Region 3, the late Dagnew W. Selassie, and Fitaye Assegu wrote a joint memorandum to Prime Minister Meles Zenawi, asking him to annul or declare invalid the redrawing of boundaries along ethnic lines.[13] To date, Meles Zenawi has not reacted one way or the other. Although information is scanty, it is now understood that the Ethiopian Patriotic Front (*Keffagne*), an underground movement for the liberation of Humera, Tselemt, Welkait, and Tsegede is now operating in the region. The TPLF, the EPLF, and others started their movements in the same way as has the *Keffagne*. These districts must be returned to their original *killils*; otherwise a bloody civil war possibly affecting the entire horn of Africa could erupt.

6.4 Ethnic Regionalism/Federalism

After the EPRDF government had been installed in Addis Ababa in May 1991, politics in Ethiopia became ethnicized. The country with 80 distinct language groups was divided into regions or *killils* along ethnic or linguistic lines. During the first decades of independence of African nations, in various political conflicts and competition for power, elites did not hesitate to make use of ethnicity. Ethnicity is an important part of the mechanism of political power. The politics of divide and rule, whose corollary is the ascription of ethnic groups, is one of the methods of government favored by despotism, African and Oriental alike.[14] As Tilahun Yilma aptly put it, "The most cynical, diabolical and destructive strategy being followed by the current (Ethiopian) regime to consolidate their power involves the divide and conquer methods."[15]

Political organizations in Ethiopia are now forced to organize along ethnic lines, while ethnic politics is banned in neighboring Eritrea. As Girma Bekele stated, "If a tribal federation were desirable, the rulers of

Eritrea would also have adopted one." He also notes, "What is going on inside Ethiopia is the transformation of a multi-ethnic society into divided, fragile, linguistic and ethnic entities to assure effective political control by the TPLF."[16]

With the introduction of ethnic politics, inter-tribal conflicts have sparked great violence in many parts of Ethiopia since 1991. The TPLF and its affiliated organizations and activists have carried out ethnic cleansing in Chercher, Gara Mulleta, Gursum, Habro, Gewane, Shashemane, Harar, Arsi, Borana, Bale, Kaffa, Wollega, Illubabor, Gondar, Wollo, and Shoa.[17] This ethnic cleansing is continuing unabated even now, although people of different ethnic origins and religious groups lived together fairly amicably before the advent of ethnic regionalism.

Today Tigrayan persons dominate both the private sector, and the government, including the courts, the police, and the armed forces. Other ethnic groups are denied fundamental legal and economic rights, including the ability to hold national political office, and to move from one region to another to look for employment opportunities. With political, economic, and military power in their hands, ethnic repression has become the norm rather than the exception. As Theodore Vestal states, "The story of Ethiopia, and the suppression of its people remains unreported or overlooked by most of the world, unlike the stories of Tibet and Burma and South Africa where astounding Nobel Peace Prize winners have vividly dramatized the plight of their people. Instead Ethiopia suffers from a conspiracy of silence."[18]

As we have seen around the world, intense ethnic conflicts have destroyed developing countries, keeping the people in turmoil and wasting their talent and energy. Regionalism is becoming a new word for apartheid and Ethiopia should not be used as a breeding ground for this extremely dangerous scheme. In Bosnia, for instance, where Serbs and Muslims had enjoyed relatively amicable relationships in the recent past, extremist leadership brought that region to ruin. Similarly, the brutal 1994 massacres in Rwanda were overwhelmingly directed from above. The government induced Hutu villagers to attack Tutsi, with whom they had lived peacefully and intermarried for many years.[19] Populist leaders fanned ethnic differences, and the result was large-scale social conflict and open civil war. The Nigerian federal system, drafted at independence in 1960, divided the country into three tribal regions. Many African countries hoped that Nigeria would be a model for the rest of Africa, but it turned out otherwise – essentially because of the divisive, unmanageable and destabilizing elements generated by its tribal elements. As former Ethiopian foreign minister, Minassie

Haile, once stated, "a similar fate is likely to await the tribal federation of Ethiopia."[20]

If Ethiopia is to avoid the horror of ethnic war, there must be a process of national reconciliation, and healing among different ethnic groups, political persuasions, and religious groups. If Ethiopians fail to meet these challenges, Ethiopians have nobody to blame but themselves. The new leaders in Ethiopia have the power and responsibility to move quickly and decisively to change the course of Ethiopian history. Crafting peaceful solutions remains one of the greatest challenges facing the new rulers. In ethnically divided Ethiopia, finding a workable medium for national reconciliation and the preservation of institutional and ethnic pluralism, as was done in South Africa, is critical to achieving peace and stability.

One may disagree with the policies of F.W. de Klerk, but one should admire his courage and vision to see the non-viability of the apartheid system, and therefore the need to dismantle it. South Africa should provide an "exit model" for those who are maintaining political authority that is at war with their own people.[21] Until recently, military dictatorships dominated most African states with limited opportunities for citizens to voice their concerns. A number of dictators have turned power over to elected civilian governments. Democratic governance is clearly the wave of the future.

For capitalism to succeed resources must be mobile. There must be free and unfettered movement of people, goods and ideas among and within regions. Pronounced seasonal unemployment has always been a problem in Ethiopia. In the past this was alleviated to some extent by temporary migration to the coffee regions and to large farms in the northwest during the harvest season. A study of temporary inter-regional migration carried out in 1969/70 indicated that places like Humera provided employment for about 100,000 people. The plantations in the Awash Valley served similar function for about 150,000 Wollo peasants. Peasants from throughout the highlands migrated to Kaffa and Sidamo to harvest coffee.[22] With ethnic regionalism, peasants in Ethiopia are being deprived from a useful source of income and severe labor shortages are created in these fast growing regions while unemployment and underemployment in the highlands persists. The Lagos Plan of Action and the World Bank's Agenda for Action called for increased trade and factor flows between neighboring countries of Africa. It is ironic that, meanwhile, Ethiopia's government is actively engaged in fragmenting the country along ethnic and linguistic lines. The current policy of ethnic regionalism is of course designed to disintegrate rather than integrate the country. It should give way to a genuinely democratic system of governance needed for economic and social development. Ethiopia has yet to develop a democratic political culture that includes a willingness to accept electoral defeat, to seek cooperation with contending factions, and a tolerance of opposition groups with other points of view.[23]

After the introduction of ethnic politics in 1991, with the creation of eight ethnic homelands *or killils*, there has been heavy rural-to-urban migration caused by inter-and intra-ethnic conflicts. Since then displaced women and children have been living in emergency camps and in street-corner, makeshift plastic-covered dwellings in urban areas. They have received some humanitarian aid from international agencies, especially in Addis Ababa, Mojo, and Nazret, in the central and southern regions, Bahr Dar and Debre Markos in the northwest, and Jimma in the southwest.[24]

According to one knowledgeable Ethiopian observer who prefers to remain anonymous:

> Persons judged to belong to the wrong ethnic group are expelled from their lands, robbed of their properties, fired from their jobs, and ordered to go back to their own ethnic state *or killil*, where the local authorities would ostensibly resettle them. The great irony of this is that the majority does not have a *killil* of their own since their grandparents left at least a generation ago.

Sources and Notes

[1] Since its beginning, the Ethiopian Peoples Revolutionary Democratic Front (EPRDF) has encouraged a proliferation of weak satellite ethnic parties that would support the objectives of the Tigrean Peoples Liberation Front (TPLF).

[2] The *modus operandi* of the TPLF has been to use the EPRDF as a front for achieving the TPLF's objectives or hegemony.

[3] Donald Crummey, *Ethnic Democracy? The Ethiopian Case*, paper presented at African Studies Association Annual Meeting, (Toronto, Canada, November 4, 1994), p. 1-2.

[4] The term, *Bantustanization*, refers to the creation of small "homelands" by an established power, with the purpose of dividing and marginalizing the people along tribal lines in order to maintain control over them.

[5] David L. Clawson and James S. Fisher, *World Regional Geography: A Development Approach, 6th Edition*, (Prentice Hall, Upper Saddle River, New Jersey, 1992), p. 283.

[6] Office of the Government Spokesperson, "Economic Reform and Development in Ethiopia," (Federal Democratic Republic of Ethiopia, Addis Ababa, January 25, 1999).

[7] Howard Handelman, *The Challenge of THIRD WORLD Development*, (Prentice Hall, Upper Saddle River, New Jersey), p. 219.

[8] Sisay Asefa, "Road Blocks to a Market Economy in Ethiopia," *Ethiopian Review*, (Ethiopian Review, Los Angeles, California, February 1996), p. 28.

[9] Theodore M. Vestal, "Plowing Under the Peasant," in *Promises Unkept: Freedom of Association in the Federal Democratic Republic of Ethiopia, Volume 2*, Paper presented at the XIII International Conference on Ethiopia, (Kyoto, Japan, 1997), p. 183.

[10] Mamo Muchie, "The Ethnic Enclosure of the Ethiopian Peasantry," *Ethiopian Register, Volume 6, No. 2*, (Ethiopian Register, Avon, Minnesota, February 1999), p. 19.

[11] Ronald Hope Kempe, Sr., *Development in the Third World: From Policy Failure to Policy Reform*, (M. E. Sharpe, Inc., Armonk, New York and London, UK, 1996) p. 176-177.

[12] *Ethiopian Register, Volume 6, No. 5*, (Ethiopian Register, Avon, Minnesota, May 1999), p. 2.

[13] The author has in his possession a copy of the Dagnew W. Selassie--Fitaye Assegu joint memorandum to Meles Zenawi.

[14] *Africa Now: People, Politics, and Institutions*, Stephen Ellis, Editor, (James Currey Ltd., London, and Heinemann, Portsmouth, New Hampshire, 1996), p. 25.

[15] Tilahun Yilma, "Ethiopia Should Secede from the Provinces of Tigray and Eritrea," *Ethiopian Review, Volume 3, No. 1*, (Ethiopian Register, Avon, Minnesota, January 1996), p. 19-22.

[16] Girma Bekele, "Mussolini Must be Laughing in His Grave," *Ethiopian Register*, Volume 2, No. 12, (Ethiopian Register, Avon, Minnesota, 1995) p. 28.

[17]*Ethiopian Register*, Volume 6, No. 5 (Ethiopian Register, Avon, Minnesota, May 1999) p. 3.

[18] Theodore M. Vestal, Speech for an Ad Hoc Committee Rally on Ethiopia, Washington, D.C., May 26, 1997.

[19] Howard Handelman, *The Challenge of THIRD WORLD Development*, (Prentice Hall, Upper Saddle River, New Jersey), p. 67.

[20] Minassie Haile, "The TPLF's Constitution for Ethiopia," *Ethiopian Register, Volume 5, No. 2*, (Ethiopian Register, Avon, Minnesota, February 1998), p. 36-43.

[21] Lual A. Deng, *Rethinking African Development: Toward a Framework for Social Integration and Ecological Harmony*, (Africa World Press Inc., Trenton, New Jersey, 1998), p. 130.

[22] Ibid, p. 134.

[23] Howard Handelman, op. cit., p. 249.

[24] *Ethiopian Register*, Volume 5, No. 5, (Ethiopian Register, Avon, Minnesota, May 1998), p. 31.

Chapter 7

The African and Regional Development Context

Africa is the poorest region in the world. Nearly all of the poorest countries of the world are African, and the gap between them and the rest of the world is growing. Ethiopia is one of the poorest of Africa's 53 countries. Four decades after independence from colonialism, African nations, including Ethiopia, are still struggling to improve the living conditions of their people. The social and economic situation in most African countries has been deteriorating since the late 1960s. Even with massive infusions of financial and technical assistance from northern-hemisphere donors, Africa is worse off today – socially, economically, environmentally, and perhaps politically, – than it was 30 years ago.[1]

The basic survival needs of most African people – clean water, good food, reasonable housing, education, and proper sanitation and health facilities – are still lacking. In fact, conditions resulting in poverty in the region are clearly getting worse. Only 15 percent of Africans today live in "an environment considered minimally adequate for sustainable growth and development." At least 45 percent of Africans live in dire poverty. African countries would need annual growth rates of seven percent or more to cut that figure in half in 15 years. In 1999, sub-Saharan Africa's economy as a whole grew by only

2.5 percent. It is likely that the next generation will be more numerous, poorer, less educated and more desperate.[2]

Two decades ago, in their widely publicized evaluation of the socio-economic situation in Africa over the two previous decades (1960-1980), African governments declared in the "Lagos Plan of Action" that Africa was in a state of underdevelopment; that the socio-economic situation in Africa was worse in 1980 than in 1960. Regretfully, the socio-economic situation has deteriorated even further since 1980.

In sub-Saharan Africa's 48 countries, the average annual growth rate has been less than three percent over the past three decades. The reasons for sub-Saharan Africa's poor economic performance are numerous. Many countries have suffered from drought, war, corrupt leadership, and ethnic conflict. Nearly all suffered from "state-led," rather than "market-oriented" economic development. Closeted behind protective trade barriers, governments borrowed money they were unable to repay, and stifled economic growth with over-regulation.

By the 1980s, the bankruptcy of the state-led approach to economic development was apparent. Then a shift to putting markets first occurred. Fiscal prudence, freer trade, privatization, and deregulation were expected to turn poor economies around by attracting private capital. Unlike Asia and Latin America, Africa failed to attract private money despite significant free-market reforms. Many countries lagged because their reforms were barely begun, in others reform was piecemeal and ineffective, or the pay-off from liberalizing reforms was slow to arrive.

In the 1990s, the importance of institutions was rediscovered. It was recognized that, for markets to work well, an economy requires a complex web of effective institutions, from basic property rights and well run legal systems to effective and uncorrupt bureaucracies. In Africa, such institutions are often weak or non-existent. Countries where property rights are weakly enforced, where the rule of law can not be counted on, and where governments are corrupt, tend to grow more slowly, even if they claim to give their citizens' capitalist impulses free rein.[3]

Wrong-headed, usually anti-market, economic policies have contributed to low levels of productive investment, poor export performance, inefficient resource use, low levels of technology, scarcity of trained manpower, high population growth rates and a strong bias against investment in agriculture. Other factors, often not entirely the fault of African governments, such as declining terms of trade, higher energy prices, severe debt burden, and high population growth rates also were constraints to economic growth.

The dismal performance of agriculture has been due to the lack of attention and resources directed at increasing the productivity of small farmers who comprise the bulk of Africa's population of nearly 800 million. In the 1960s, Africa was virtually self-sufficient in food production with a growth rate of about 2.3 percent a year, roughly the same as the population growth rate at that time. In the 1970s, however, growth in food production dropped to around one percent a year while the population grew at about three percent. With the decline in food production, food imports to Africa increased greatly. During the decade of the 1970s, food imports to Africa grew at an average annual rate of 8.4 percent. Approximately US$5 billion has been spent annually for imported food consumed by African people during most of the past three decades.[4]

7.1 The Lagos Plan of Action for Africa[5]

Confronted with the harsh African reality of underdevelopment, essentially characterized by persistent mass poverty, African Heads of States and Governments adopted the "Lagos Plan of Action" in Lagos, Nigeria, in 1980. It attributed the origins of Africa's underdevelopment to be outside the control of Africa's leaders. Rather its origins were attributed to the legacy of integration into the world economic system on unequal terms that commenced with colonial exploitation. This was due to the structure of the international economy, and continued unequal terms of exchange with the developed world.[6] It provided a plan for Africa's development over the period 1980-2000. The Lagos Plan reaffirmed Africa's twin principles of establishing a common market and enhancing national and collective self-reliance and self-sustaining development. The governments of Africa also decided and stated in the Lagos Plan of Action, that they would depend mainly upon themselves, individually and collectively, for pulling their African economies out of deepening crisis and reversing the trend of African underdevelopment. It was intended to be the guiding document for African nations in the 1980s, and was endorsed by United Nations agencies, including the World Bank. With regard to the food problem in Africa, the Lagos Plan called for a three-pronged basic policy approach:

- African governments should direct much greater resources into agriculture.

- African governments should re-orient their respective social systems to ensure consistency with the promotion of rural development, particularly through increases in the productivity levels of small producers via agricultural cooperatives.
- African governments should promote agriculture within the context of their respective national socio-economic plans.

Unfortunately, the Lagos Plan gathered dust and by the end of the decade of the 1980s conditions had deteriorated beyond the imagination of even the worst pessimist. The post-independence optimism of African countries of the 1960s had not lasted long. The poverty situation in Africa had reached a crisis point that continued to worsen through the 1990s. The major issues of the 21st century will be how these impediments to sustainable development can be overcome, self-confidence gained, and human rights for all citizens guaranteed. Attainment of sustainable development in Africa requires, *inter alia*, regional economic integration as already envisioned in the Lagos Plan's proposed African Economic Community. That proposal was directed at promoting the collective, accelerated, self-reliant and self-sustaining development of member states, cooperation among these states and their economic integration.[7]

Its goal was to be achieved in two stages. During the first stage, the decade of the 1980s, the objective was to strengthen the existing regional economic communities, and to establish economic groupings in the other regions so as to cover the continent as a whole. During the second stage, the decade of the 1990s, sectoral integration was to be further strengthened, and measures taken towards the progressive establishment of a common market. To this end, four regional organizations were established to cover the continent. These are the Economic Community of West African States (ECOWAS) with 16 member states, promulgated in Lagos in May 1975; the Preferential Trade Area for Eastern and Southern Africa (PTA-ESA) with 16 member states, promulgated in Lusaka in December 1981; the Economic Community of Central African States (CEEAC) with ten member states, promulgated in Libreville in October 1983; and the States Union of the Arab Maghreb (SUAM) with five member states, promulgated in Marakech in February 1989.[8]

Critics argue that this approach has been generally unsuccessful because the model drawn from industrialized Western Europe was not applicable to Africa. They believe that the requisites for integration do not presently exist in Africa, but must be created. In Western Europe, the Common Market was created after industrialization, and when productivity in the agricultural sector had increased enough to produce a surplus over the subsistence needs of the agrarian population. They maintain that only when such a surplus has become available can the process of transfer to the industrial sector be initiated. In contrast, economies in Africa can be characterized by low levels of productivity, widespread poverty, hunger, and semi-subsistence production. Furthermore, many believe that the great diversity of Africa's nation states has contributed to failed efforts at economic integration. African countries differ from one another in many ways including:

- Institutional deficiencies.
- Politico-ideological factors.
- External dependence.
- Stage of development.
- Religious, linguistic and ethnic factors.
- Uneven distribution of potential benefits and costs of integration.[9]

Given these constraints, prospects of any significant bilateral free trade, let alone a common market or economic union in the foreseeable future is unlikely. It is difficult to imagine that Africa will have a common market soon in the face of its continuing economic stagnation, not to mention political and social instability.

7.2 The World Bank's Agenda for Action [10]

In the fall of 1979, the African Governors of the World Bank addressed a memorandum to the Bank's President, Robert McNamara, expressing their alarm at the dim economic prospects for the nations of Sub-Saharan Africa. They requested that the Bank prepare, "a special paper on the economic development problems of these countries and an appropriate program for helping them." The findings of the World Bank's 1981 report, entitled, "Accelerated Development in Sub-Saharan Africa: An Agenda for Action," were critical of the strategies pursued by African governments in the 1960s and 1970s. It blamed the economic crisis primarily on the performance of African governments and discounted the role of exogenous factors, e.g., deterioration in terms of trade – even though it is clear that both internal and external factors had greatly contributed to Africa's economic crises. [11]

It built its recommendations on the Bank's own experience in Africa, as well as Asia and Latin America. Unlike the Lagos Plan, the

World Bank stressed domestic economic policy reform, but it endorsed self-reliance and a more integrated continent by the year 2000. In this endeavor, the Bank believed that all nations could collaborate in defining options and the alternatives for tapping the vast potential of the African continent. The Bank further argued that the ultimate decisions must, however, be for the nations of Africa alone to make. Indeed, before external donors could help, Africa needed to address its own complex problems with energy, intelligence, and integrity. That was the sober message of the World Bank's report. [12]

The "Agenda for Action" policies and priorities in agriculture included the following:

- Focus on smallholder production.
- Changing incentive structures by raising producer prices.
- Developing more open and competitive marketing arrangements.
- Involving farmers in the decisions that affect them.
- Expanding agricultural research.
- Undertaking quick-yielding activities in irrigated agriculture. [13]

7.3 The World Bank's From Crisis to Sustainable Growth [14]

In 1989, the World Bank undertook another even more in depth study of sub-Saharan Africa entitled, "Sub-Saharan Africa: From Crisis to Sustainable Growth." It was intended to be used by policymakers in Africa and in the development community as a resource on which to draw in the task of formulating specific long-term country development strategies for the 1990s. It recognized that most African countries had embarked on comprehensive programs of economic adjustment and that these programs had evolved with experience and mistakes. The study urged continued adjustment efforts and broadened and deepened reform with special measures to alleviate poverty and protect vulnerable people in African societies.

To achieve food security, provide jobs, and register a modest improvement in living standards, it called for sub-Saharan economies to grow by at least four to five percent a year. And for growth to be sustainable, it stressed that major efforts must be made to protect, not destroy, the environment. It recognized that agriculture must be the main foundation for growth, at least during the 1990s; that food production must increase twofold for Africa to cope with the new mouths to be fed and overcome malnutrition. The key to food security was seen as the development and dissemination of new technologies, as well as efforts to slow the population growth rate. A central theme of the study was that, although sound macroeconomic policies and an efficient infrastructure are essential to provide an enabling environment for the productive use of resources, they alone are not sufficient to transform the structure of African economies. At the same time major efforts are needed to build African capacities – to produce a better trained, more healthy population and to greatly strengthen the institutional framework within which development can take place.

The root cause of weak economic performance in the past was identified as the failure of public institutions. It concluded that private sector initiative and market mechanisms are important, but they must go hand-in-hand with good governance – a public service that is efficient, a judicial system that is reliable, and a government administration that is accountable to its public. It called for a better balance between the government and the governed, and set out a range of proposals aimed at empowering ordinary people, especially women, to take greater responsibility for improving their lives. It recommended measures to foster grassroots organization and nurture, rather than obstruct, informal sector enterprises, and non-governmental and intermediary organizations. The study urged that development be more bottom-up and less top-down. It strongly supported faster progress toward regional economic cooperation and integration, a central theme of the "Lagos Plan of Action" and the African Development Bank's 1989 "African Development Report."

7.4 The ECA's Special Memorandum on Africa's Economic and Social Crisis[15]

With the persistence of the socio-economic crisis in Africa, at its 1984 Conference of Ministers, the ECA produced a "Special Memorandum on African's Economic and Social Crisis." The ECA memorandum analyzed the crisis and presented some policy suggestions to address the crisis, including the following:

- Mobilization and optimal utilization of scarce resources.
- Provision of adequate incentives for producers.

- Improvement of national institutional and administrative structures.
- Promotion of entrepreneurial development.
- Sensitization and mobilization of entire populations to ensure effective participation in implementation and reconstruction efforts.
- Implementation of policies directed at achieving socio-economic equity and justice.

The ECA memorandum proposed essentially the same approaches as those contained in the "Lagos Plan of Action." The approaches stressed the adoption of measures to structurally transform African economies and the pursuit of policies for strengthening sub-regional and regional cooperation within the context of promoting individual state and collective self-reliance. To date, African countries have been unable to transform African economies, nor have they been able to strengthen sub-regional and regional cooperation as articulated in the "Lagos Plan of Action" and the other documents discussed in this chapter. Individual state or collective self-reliance within the foreseeable future appears to be unrealistic.

7.5 Africa: The Challenge of Economic Recovery and Accelerated Development[16]

The ECA Conference on *Africa: The Challenge of Economic Recovery and Accelerated Development* was held in Aruba, Nigeria, in June 1987. It was convened pursuant to the United Nations General Assembly Special Session on African development of May 1986 that unanimously adopted a "Program of Action for African Development." Building on earlier UN and UN/ECA studies, the Aruba Conference with its papers and subsequent 796-page report were intended to provide a total picture of the African development experience with guidance for the future to assist African countries and international donors.

Its measures for *accelerating the recovery process* included:

Sustaining domestic policy reforms and improvement in economic management – African countries must continue to pursue structural policy reform measures, taking into account the need to minimize the adverse social impact of such measures and the human dimension of adjustment. They must continue to ensure that the budgetary cuts do not affect the development of social infrastructure, particularly health and education; and put greater emphasis on the rationalization of government institutions to ensure an effective and efficient public sector contribution to the recovery process. African governments must create favorable conditions for decentralization of decision-making, and delegation of authority and responsibility for increased access to resources so as to broaden the participation of all groups of the population in the recovery process.

Structural adjustment program and the recovery process – African countries must sustain and accelerate the process of economic recovery by increasing the level of investment in agriculture, developing rural transportation with greater emphasis on low-cost transport equipment and promoting agro-allied industries. They must ensure that structural adjustment programs are consistent with the requirements for recovery and growth. They are urged to undertake, with the assistance of African regional institutions, concerted efforts to exchange information on their negotiations with international financial organizations and donors on policy reform measures and structural adjustment programs. They must also take appropriate measures for controlling capital flight and the brain drain from Africa.

With regard to *debt and debt service payments* – In view of the severity of the debt-servicing problem in many countries in Africa and its dire implications for recovery and development prospects, new efforts will be needed to deal with this problem, particularly in so far as low-income countries are concerned. These efforts should include:

- Lower interest rates, longer repayments, and grace periods to reduce the debt-service burden.
- Conversion into grants of bilateral government-to-government debt and interest obligations for low-income countries undertaking structural adjustment programs where this has not already been accomplished.
- Repayment of debt in local currency should be considered.
- Conversion of debt and debt servicing obligations into investment portfolios and equity.

With regard to *development assistance* – The Conference emphasized the "urgent need for increased aid flows that would provide the resources required for recovery and development."

With regard to *commodities, trade, and price stabilization* – The Conference recognized the benefits of intra-African trade, and strengthening existing international cooperation in commodities. It recognized the linkage between commodities, price levels, external debt, and the need for international resource flows. It also noted the marked rigidities in the trade policies of industrialized countries toward Africa; a trend which proved detrimental to Africa's efforts to shift away from commodity dependence.

With regard to *political and economic destabilization and the consequences for economic recovery and development* – The Conference recognized that peace, security and stability are necessary pre-conditions for Africa's economic development.

On the *prospects for long-term development* – The Conference concluded that Africa needs a new approach to its political economy. This should involve more coherent and more clearly thought out principles to guide its development process and to provide a framework for more efficient resource mobilization. In this context, recovery must also mean economic reconstruction for long-term development which, in turn calls for new forms of social organization and economic management, and the bridging of economic and social disparities. The Conference therefore decided to forward the following recommendations to all African countries:

- Internalization of the productive forces and the growth impetus, as well as increased and effective self-reliance and cooperation on a regional basis.
- Intensification of popular participation in the economic development process and the promotion of social justice and distributive equity.
- Recognition of the fundamental role of women in the development process.
- Development and enhancement of African research and the encouragement of the process of technological and scientific innovation and adaptation.
- Ensure consistency of the development process and environmental sustainability.
- Greater reliance on African technical and scientific skills and entrepreneurship.
- Political, social, administrative and cultural dimensions that are conducive to long-term development must be created to ensure the success and sustainability of the development process.

With regard to *economic cooperation in Africa and between Africa and the international community* – To reverse the disappointing experience with economic integration and to ensure that the process of integration contributes more effectively to economic development and structural change, the Conference recommended:

- African countries should embark on a comprehensive approach to economic integration involving the rationalization of existing cooperation organs in each sub-region, and their effective mobilization for coordinated planning and development at the sub-regional level.
- They should pursue measures for the close coordination of economic and social policies at the sub-regional level as well as for the joint planning and development of community projects in the key economic sectors.
- The current effort to harmonize the activities of the multinational institutions established under the aegis of OAU and ECA should be accelerated with a view to ensuring that their institutions act in support of the comprehensive approach to economic cooperation and integration.
- The comprehensive approach to economic cooperation should be accompanied by new efforts to promote closer collaboration with other developing regions. In particular, the newly industrializing countries are now in a position to provide African countries with an effective program of technical cooperation in support of sectoral planning at the sub-regional level in the key economic sectors.
- Realizing that, in the final analysis, the pursuit of self-reliant and self-sustaining development on the continent would demand a new pattern of economic relationship with the developed countries involving new trade structures and new efforts to promote foreign investment in Africa, African countries should devise appropriate mechanisms for promoting collaboration between the different productive sectors in Africa and those in the developed countries.

Although it was highly touted a decade ago as comprehensive and significant guidance for African development efforts into the decade of the 1990s, like many earlier African regional efforts the "Program of Action for African Development" had little apparent impact on African regional development or individual African country development.

7.6 The Harare Declaration Re: Africa's Food Security Crisis[17]

The "Harare Declaration on the Food Crisis in Africa" was adopted in mid-1984 at the FAO Regional Conference for Africa. The declaration called for the promotion of self-reliance, food and agricultural production, food security and external assistance for Africa. The specific recommendations of the Harare Declaration were:

- Allocation of adequate resources to support agricultural production at all levels with special emphasis on smallholders.
- Establishment of an improved incentive system through more remunerative producer prices; more efficient marketing systems; sufficient and timely supply of inputs and of consumer goods; and greater involvement of farmers in decision making.
- Provision of credit facilities and timely payment of farmers' entitlements.
- Improvement in the implementation of existing programs and projects, and rehabilitation of existing infrastructure, including irrigation and rural roads.
- Intensification of training and research including, in particular, the granting of scholarships for studies or research in countries on appropriate technologies in crops, livestock, fisheries and forestry.
- Expansion of pest control and related activities and measures to reduce post-harvest losses.
- Eradication of animal diseases and pests such as rinderpest and typanosomiasis.
- Increased financial and material assistance from international organizations and donor agencies to accelerate agricultural development in the region.

Pursuant to the Harare Declaration at the 1984 FAO Regional Conference for Africa, the UN General Assembly adopted an urgent resolution on the then current emergency food situation in African countries. That resolution focused on facilitating adequate food production, and maximizing stability in the flow of food supplies to points where required, ensuring physical and economic access for all those in need, whether countries, families or individuals.

7.7 Donor Trends and Issues in Africa

In the 1950s and 1960s, the development aims of African governments, and bilateral and multilateral donors all had a mutual preoccupation with basic infrastructure and institution building. In the 1970s, this mutual concern shifted to a focus on providing aid to the rural areas where most of the people lived and worked to improve infrastructure, education, and health services. This was referred to as the era of the "basic human needs" approach.

Then in the 1980s, there was a shift away from "basic human needs" to policy reform and support for agricultural development (particularly food self-sufficiency) by both the bilateral and multilateral donors. In the 1990s, donor support for policy reform continued, with less attention to agriculture, and more attention to good governance, private sector, and human resources development, including efforts to combat HIV-AIDS. Also debt forgiveness and the opening up of western markets for African exports have received increased attention.[18]

Many African government leaders have been reluctant to support the policy reform and improved governance priorities of the donors over the past two decades. They blame Africa's failures on excessive debt owed to donors, exploitative trading relations, and too-strict demands for economic reform. They do agree, at least rhetorically, on the major priorities for Africa's development: aid for balance of payments, and long-term development based on population planning, agricultural development and related development of human resources and non-agricultural sectors.

But they do not agree on the implementation of policies and programs that impinge upon their personalizing and maintaining power that undermines, rather than builds, national institutions. The African state and its president are often viewed as one and the same. Most African presidents make no distinction between their party and government, using the panoply of government offices in the election campaigns. There are elections in Africa, but little democracy. The donors, whose support often is essential for African rulers, demand multi-party democracy on a western model. Yet donors demands for democracy have been inconsistent. Especially for the first 30 years of

African independence, prior to the end of the cold war in 1990, western donors and the USSR supported often greedy and corrupt dictators in an effort to keep their allegiance.[19]

In the 1980s and to a lesser degree in the 1990s, the International Monetary Fund (IMF) and World Bank led the donors' effort to encourage policy reforms and implement structural adjustment programs in African countries and around the world. This effort rightly focused on opening and strengthening markets. It assumed competitive market forces, unimpeded by government intervention, would lead to the best possible pattern of resource allocation. African governments were urged to adopt austerity measures, privatize state-owned industries, and generally develop democratic market economies open to world competition. In particular, African governments were encouraged to seek private foreign investment and expand exports – wherever possible including labor-intensive manufacturing – to serve as an engine for growth. Regretfully, unlike so many Asian and Latin American countries, some African countries that implemented the policy reform packages proposed by the IMF and World Bank suffered disastrous consequences. In retrospect, while structural adjustment produced some real gains in some countries, the various priority reforms should have been implemented sequentially. Often, too many reforms were introduced simultaneously and then were implemented either too vigorously or not vigorously enough. In other instances, reforms were implemented piecemeal. Also attention should have been given to building institutions to support a market-led economy, e.g., protection of basic property rights, effective legal systems, and bureaucracies that are less corrupt.[20]

Critics maintain that the IMF and World Bank required African governments to adopt policies that pushed millions of Africans still deeper into the mire of poverty and dependency. As one observer put it, "The IMF uses Africa as a laboratory for its economic experiments. Impoverished African governments with a gun at their head often give in to pressure and allow the IMF to dictate their economic policy. With so many Africans fighting other Africans, the continent has lost control over its future. The IMF is seen as imposing on them an economic orthodoxy which is against their interests and indeed violates their sovereignty through the conditions it attaches to loans."[21] There was evidence that stabilization and structural adjustment programs were rending the fabric of some African societies in the 1980s. Worse still, their severest impact was on the vulnerable groups in society – children, women and the aged – who constitute two-thirds of the population.

As a condition of support from the IMF and World Bank, African countries had to implement macro-policies that would open and strengthen market economies and promote world trade, regardless of the short and long-term consequences. Such policies were intended to:

- Reduce budget deficits through an immediate reduction in public expenditures.
- Eliminate all forms of price and wage controls, including the removal of subsidies on basic foodstuffs that often formed an essential part of the bargain between governments and key interest groups.
- Control the money supply.
- Devalue the currency in order to promote exports and reduce imports and remove tariffs and quotas that protect infant third-world industries.[22]

7.8 An Alternative Development Strategy

Although the "basic human needs" approach has not been in vogue for some two decades, there is much to be said for its application in Africa. People need food, water, proper sanitation and health facilities, shelter, and education. The basic human needs approach is one which gives priority to meeting the basic needs of all the people. The basic human needs strategy consists of both a radical and a liberal version. While the central issue for the radical version is redistributing power, the liberal version is concerned with directly coping with poverty. According to one interpretation, the basic human needs approach is revolutionary because it calls for radical redistribution, not only of incomes and assets but also of power, and for the political mobilization of the poor themselves. At the other extreme, the approach has been interpreted as a minimum welfare sop to keep the poor quiet. An intermediate interpretation is that basic human needs have been met by a variety of political regimes and that revolution is neither a necessary nor a sufficient condition.[23]

There are at least three steps that are essential to formulating a basic human needs-oriented development strategy. First, the target groups must be defined with a good deal of precision after collecting the necessary data on the profile of poverty within these countries. Second, quantitative studies must be undertaken to estimate the percent of the population below the minimum level of basic human needs, and estimate the investment and production requirements to meet consumption needs over a defined period of time. Third, the necessary policy and program instruments of implementation should be defined to indicate how investment and production will result in consumption targets being realized, even in a market where demand signals may all be pointing in a different direction.

Related to the basic human needs approach, an effective economic and social development strategy must call for local people's participation in planning and implementing development efforts that affect their lives and livelihood. The World Bank's "Agenda for Action" recommended community participation in decisions that affect their lives and interests as did the 1990 "African Charter for Popular Participation in Development." In a rare consensus, the Charter attested to the fact that, "people's participation must be at the heart of Africa's development mission and vision," and it confirmed that, "authentic development springs from the collective imagination, experience and decision of people." Following the above declaration, the United Nations Economic Commission for Africa (ECA), took some preliminary steps to promote popular participation in development in the Africa region, but the promotion of popular participation in development planning has been very slow and piecemeal due to lack of sufficient funding.[24]

Both the policy reform-structural adjustment and the basic human needs approaches should be considered by policy decision-makers in African countries in formulating their own, "country specific" development strategies. Such "country specific" strategies should contain elements of both approaches that improve levels of living of the ordinary, long-suffering people, most of whom are rural families. The lessons learned from the application of these strategies to date can provide the guidance needed to avoid the mistakes of the past four decades. The basic human needs approach should improve levels of living in the near term, while the policy reform and structural adjustment measures to create a vibrant well-working market economy are being implemented over the long term.

7.9 The Importance of Smallholder Agriculture

The importance of smallholder agriculture in the economic life of African countries was stressed in the "Lagos Plan of Action," the World Bank's "Agenda for Action" and "From Crisis to Sustainable Development," as well as the various other studies of African economic and social development. It should be noted that some countries, such as Kenya, had given priority to smallholder agriculture long before and succeeded in improving the levels of living of rural people. From 1955 until 1972, agricultural production in Kenya increased by four percent per annum and much of that growth came from small farmer production. The major reason for the jump in production was the introduction of high-yielding varieties of hybrid corn. Similarly, smallholder tea and coffee production in Kenya grew from a negligible amount in the early 1960s to one-third of total production in the 1970s.

Although smallholder production has been widely recognized for at least three decades as the engine of economic growth by development scholars and practitioners, there is little evidence, even today, that small farmers' needs are receiving adequate attention in the majority of African states.[25] The capital and foreign exchange required for significant investment in agriculture are still too small. Failure to invest adequately in agriculture and other parts of the food system has choked off the process of structural transformation and hunger alleviation. The process of small farmer development requires greater human and capital investment, and the development and widespread diffusion of new agricultural technology. Unfortunately, most African governments simply do not have adequate resources to implement any serious development strategy. Agricultural funding from the African Development Bank has been very limited. Private international banks make few investments in African agricultural production programs because of the high risk and administrative costs. Investment in African agriculture by the World Bank and other multilateral and bilateral donor agencies has declined precipitously since the mid-1980s. Although external capital investment is important, it is clear that even more domestic private capital must be created and mobilized in each country to address this major need.[26]

Irrigated agriculture has been identified by both the OAU and the World Bank as important to solving Africa's food problem. Irrigation projects have obvious appeal as they address the vagaries of inadequate or erratic rainfall. However, large-scale drainage and irrigation projects require very heavy capital expenditures. Costs run as high as US$30,000 per hectare, a staggering amount of investment for national governments and external donors. In addition to cost overruns, institutional factors and the policy environment for irrigation are important determinants of the success or failure of individual projects. Specifically, institutions to operate and maintain public irrigated schemes, availability of inputs, adequate budgetary resources, accessible markets, reasonable producer prices, and adequate physical infrastructure are necessary conditions frequently not met in African countries. Therefore the role of large-scale irrigated agriculture is limited. Nonetheless, each country agricultural strategy should consider what role that irrigated agriculture can play in a given situation. Special emphasis should be given to the prospects for small-scale private irrigated agricultural systems as these have proven in the past to have the best results.[27]

Sources and Notes

[1] Ronald Hope Kempe, Sr., *Development in the Third World: From Policy Failure to Policy Reform*, (M. E. Sharpe, Inc., Armonk, New York and London, UK, 1996), p. 153.

[2] See "Africa - The heart of the matter," (*The Economist*, May 13, 2000), p. 22.

[3] For further discussion, see "Time to roll out a new model," (*The Economist*, March 1, 1997), p. 71-72. Also see Jeffrey Sachs, "Growth in Africa: It can be done," (*The Economist*, June 29, 1996), p. 19-21.

[4] Togba-Nah Tipoten, "Dimensions of the Rural Crisis in Africa," paper presented at FAO Conference on Agrarian Reform, Rome, (FAO, Rome, 1988), p. 6.

[5] OAU, *The Lagos Plan of Action - for the Implementation of the Monrovia Strategy for the Economic Development of Africa*, adopted by the Second Extraordinary Assembly of the OAU Head of States and Governments devoted to economic matters, Lagos, Nigeria, April 28-29, 1980 (OAU, Addis Ababa, 1980).

[6] For obvious reasons, the African Heads of States and Governments' "Lagos Plan" did not address the effects of war, corrupt leadership, tribal conflicts, or wrong-headed economic policies on Africa's progress in economic and social development.

[7] Ann Seidman and Frederick Anang, Editors, *21st Century Africa – Towards a new Vision of Self-Sustainable Development*, (African Studies Association Press and Africa World Press Inc, Trenton New Jersey, 1992), p. 88.

[8] Ibid., p. 71.

[9] Ann Seidman and Frederick Anang, op.cit., p. 88-92.

[10] World Bank, *Accelerated Development in Sub-Saharan Africa: An Agenda for Action*, (The World Bank, Washington, D.C., 1981).

[11] Ibid., p. 1-44.

[12] For an in-depth discussion of the OAU and World Bank documents, see *Africa in Economic Crisis,* John Ravenhill, Editor, (Columbia University Press, New York, 1986).

[13] World Bank, op.cit., p. 45-80.

[14] World Bank, *Sub-Saharan Africa: From Crisis to Sustainable Growth*, (The World Bank, Washington, D.C., 1989).

[15] ECA/UN, *Special Memorandum by the ECA Conference of Ministers on Africa's Economic and Social Crisis*, May 24-28, 1984, (Economic Commission for Africa/United Nations, Addis Ababa, Ethiopia, 1984).

[16] Adebayo Adedeji, Owodunni Teriba and Patrick Bugembe, Editors, *The Challenge of African Economic Recovery and Development*, papers prepared for the ECA-organized International Conference on "Africa: the Challenge of Economic Recovery and Accelerated Development," held in Aruba, Nigeria on June 15-19 1987, (Frank Cass & Co, Ltd., London), p. 783-796.

[17] FAO/UN, *Report of the Thirteenth FAO Regional Conference for Africa*, held in Harare, Zimbabwe, July 16-25, 1984, (Food and Agricultural Organization/United Nations, Rome, 1984).

[18] During the 1990s, the debt burden of sub-Saharan African nations was reduced by at least US$11 billion. There is concern that in some countries creating a fresh balance sheet benefits corrupt leaders, as well as Russian and Ukrainian arms-dealers. See "Africa - The heart of the matter," (*The Economist*, May 13, 2000), p. 22-24.

[19] See Robert J. Berg, "Foreign Aid in Africa: Here's the Answer – Is It Relevant to the Question?" Chapter 18 in *Strategies for African Development, "* (University of California Press, Berkeley 1986), p. 505-543. Also see "Africa: the heart of the matter," (*The Economist*, May 13, 2000), p. 22-24.

[20] See Jeffrey Sachs, op.cit., p. 19-21.

[21] Kofi Buenor Hadjor, *Africa in an Era of Crisis*, (Africa World Press Inc., Trenton, New Jersey, 1990), p. 218.

[22] Susan and Peter Calvert, *Politics and Society in the Third World – An Introduction*, (Harvester Wheatsheaf Prentice Hall, 1996), p. 100-101.

[23] Ben Wisner, *Power and Need in Africa*, (Africa World Press Inc., Trenton, New Jersey, 1989), p. 41.

[24] ECA/UN, *Poverty Alleviation and Environmental Conservation*, A Training Manual, No. 4, (Economic Commission for Africa/United Nations, Addis Ababa, Ethiopia, 1993), p. 1.

[25] For a recent appraisal, see Derek Byerlee and Lane E. Holdcroft, *The Role of Cooperation from the North in Strengthening Human and Institutional Capital to Support Rural Development in Africa: With a Focus on the Agricultural Knowledge Triangle*, Paper presented at a special session entitled, "Strengthening Human and Institutional Capital to Support Rural Development in Africa: What Have We Learned and What Are the Challenges?" (XXIV International Conference of Agricultural Economists, Berlin, Germany, August 12, 2000).

[26] Organisation for Economic Co-operation and Development (OECD), *The DAC Journal: Development Cooperation Report 1999, International Development, Efforts and Policies of Members of the Development Assistance Committee*, (OECD Development Assistance Committee, Paris, 2000).

[27] Andra P Thakur, "Technological Transfer and the Failure of Nigeria's Green Revolution," in *Sustainable Agriculture in Africa*, E. Ann McDougall,

Editor, (Africa World Press Inc., Trenton, New Jersey, 1990), p. 49. Also see Shawki Barghouti and Guy Le Moigne, *Irrigation in Sub-Saharan Africa: The Development of Public and Private Systems,* World Bank Technical Paper Number 123, (The World Bank, Washington, D.C., 1990), p. vii-ix.

Chapter 8

Agricultural Credit in the Rural Subsistence Sector

Economic activities in the Ethiopian rural subsistence sector center principally on grain crops, livestock, forestry, poultry, handicrafts, and small-scale cottage industries. Small production units with average holdings of about two hectares characterize the dominant smallholder agricultural sector. Agriculture remains the most important source of food, raw materials, government revenues, foreign exchange earnings, and employment. Yet agricultural production has been declining since the 1960s, while the rate of population growth has been steadily rising. Evidence of the failure of the agricultural sector to satisfy the demand for food is indicated by import statistics. Between 1975 and 1980, the real value of imports of food and live animals rose from US$2.6 million US$8.8 million, an average annual growth rate of over 22 per cent. During the same period, the food-import share of foreign exchange expenditures rose from 2.7 percent to 4.2 percent. Since 1980, food imports and the food-import share of foreign exchange expenditures have continued at very high levels.[1] The long-term decline in agricultural output can be attributed to a number of factors. Particularly noteworthy is the lack of attention and resources directed at raising the productivity of smallholder agriculture. A significant example of neglect is the woefully inadequate amount of agricultural credit made available to the rural subsistence smallholder, and the total neglect of encouraging   savings   mobilization   by   successive   Ethiopian governments.

8.1   Savings Mobilization

It has been argued that the rural population is poor and cannot save given their limited subsistence incomes. It has also been argued that external financial assistance in the form of cheap subsidized credit was necessary to improve and transform rural economies. These have both been categorically disproved. Evidence from countries around the world, including Brazil, the Republic of China, the Republic of Korea, Pakistan, Bangladesh, and Zambia, indicate that the rural poor can and do save, provided they are given proper incentives. Rural households have a substantial savings capacity when they have attractive investment opportunities, but this capacity needs to be promoted and strengthened through national savings campaigns and educational efforts.[2] Savings may take many forms ranging from monetary assets such as cash, bank savings deposits and other liquid assets, to real assets such as crop inventories, land, jewelry, and labor services. Third world countries are often encouraged to increase their savings ratio as a necessary step for achieving growth. Increases in the savings ratio are expected to lead to education and an understanding of dependence on foreign aid, to which there are always some strings attached. Mobilized savings on the other hand can be transformed into productive uses in the form of rural credit to assist in the adoption of technological innovations, expanding production, and improving consumption.[3] Traditionally, savings mobilized in rural areas have been re-lent primarily in urban areas, where higher interest rates prevailed.

A well-known FAO credit specialist argues that to make savings a more effective instrument for development, it must be linked to formal financial markets. For this to occur, he suggests the following incentives:

- The creation of convenient savings channels for beneficiaries.
- Safety and accessibility of deposits.
- Attempt to develop the best possible deposit and withdrawal arrangements at lowest possible cost to the saver.
- An attractive yield or interest rate on those savings.[4]

Higher rates of interest will induce people to increase savings further in the form of deposits and bonds rather than divert those savings toward the purchase of gold, jewelry or hoards of foreign exchange. Low interest rates may also divert potential savings toward less useful investment. Increased mobilization of savings in the rural areas would necessarily entail having access to saving and lending facilities. However, as a result of an urban bias in development policy, most financial institutions are currently concentrated in the urban areas and centers of population much to the neglect of rural areas. Financial institutions need to branch out into the rural areas to allow rural residents access to such institutions. In other words, the rural money markets need to be tapped, not only through the traditional local branch establishment, but also through offering appropriate savings and credit instruments suited to the needs of the rural population.[5]

The creation of a regular and minimum savings habit is indispensable for development at all levels, including that of the individual family. Rural people should, therefore, be encouraged to make regular savings in order to accelerate the savings process, to reinforce the savings habit, and to strengthen group commitment and solidarity. The two usual types of savings are informal voluntary and contractual savings. In informal voluntary savings, group members pledge to save voluntarily on a regular, usually weekly, basis. These savings are generally deposited with the group treasurer each time a group meets. The members decide where and how often they should meet. In contractual savings, ten percent of the total loan is deducted and saved by the group with the lending institution as a condition for receiving the loan. Although assistance from outside sources can always be obtained, the principle of self-reliance implies that the group must be able to mobilize funds from within to enable it to carry out its necessary minimal functions.

8.2 Sources of Rural Credit in Ethiopia

The Informal Financial Sector: Most of the credit that is available to the Ethiopian subsistence sector comes from the informal financial sector. Some 93 percent of the small farmers in Ethiopia either do not borrow or depend on the private moneylender. Though accurate data is difficult to find, it is estimated that about one percent of the total number of farmers use institutional credit. The bulk of agricultural loans emanate from non-institutional sources such as the private moneylender, other farmers, middlemen, neighbors, friends, relatives, and merchants. The interest rates on such loans are very high. In the Chilalo Agricultural Development Unit (CADU), for instance, before the launching of the project in 1967, the interest rate charged by the private moneylender was between 50 and 100 percent. However, after the project was operational, it declined to only 12 percent. Because of the collateral requirements, small farmers are forced to borrow from informal sources. The private moneylender is not involved in savings mobilization efforts, concentrating on only providing credit. Informal sources of credit have the advantage of adaptability, organizational flexibility, popular participation, easy accessibility, and relatively low operational costs.[6] Most of the credit that is available to farmers in developing countries is short-term for one crop season or for one or two years. Such loans are in cash or in kind. Collateral security for loans takes many forms, ranging from land mortgages, liens on crops, personal guarantors, to formal promissory notes.

Formal Financial Institutions: Formal financial institutions operating in Ethiopia are largely urban-based and urban-oriented, with their clientele almost exclusively in the domain of urban merchants and traders. These institutions include the National Bank of Ethiopia (the Central Bank), the Commercial Bank of Ethiopia, and the Agricultural and Industrial Development Bank (AIDB). Since 1992, four privately owned banks with 33 branches have opened and become operational. These are the Bank of Abyssinia, the Awash International Bank, the Dashen Bank, and the Wegagen Bank. These institutions are characterized by their profit motives, little or no rural savings mobilization efforts, and inadequate provision of credit to the rural subsistence sector. Their insistence on loans to individuals and physical collateral for securing agricultural loans has impeded the expansion of agricultural credit services to small farmers.[7]

The major institutions with rural outreach are:

The Commercial Bank of Ethiopia – As noted previously, the Commercial Bank of Ethiopia, constitutes the core of the Ethiopian financial services system. This institution was created with its only motive to make profit, and has had inadequate provision of credit and savings mobilization in the rural areas. The Commercial Bank has traditionally channeled most of its loans to other sectors of the Ethiopian economy, and has been reluctant to deal with subsistence agriculture. It has a poor record in making loans available to agriculture because of its emphasis on collateral requirements rather than the productive capacity of small farmers. Land is the most acceptable form of security, and tenants have no land or other security to offer. Even after the 1975 land reform proclamation that made all rural lands the "collective property" of Ethiopians, land title remained in the hands of the government. Since tenants have only a usufruct right to the land, obtaining loans by using land as collateral was out of the question.[8] The other problem was the high (25 percent) interest rate charged by the Commercial Bank. Credit worthiness was thus largely confined to those larger landowners or those who had a salary.[9]

Since the Commercial Bank already has an extensive network of more than 100 rural branches, it has the potential to provide credit services to most of rural Ethiopia without the cost and delay associated with building a new institution. Creating a more flexible set of rules and regulations under which credit can be granted and savings mobilized is a necessary first step in realizing that potential. Providing access to credit further encourages private investment. The Commercial Bank should therefore be encouraged to innovate and to move away from its traditional orientation. The best way of achieving this is through preferential rediscount rates, used on a temporary basis to familiarize it with agricultural lending.

The Agricultural and Industrial Development Bank (AIDB) – The Agricultural and Industrial Development Bank was established in the early 1950s by merging the Development Bank of Ethiopia and the Ethiopia Investment Corporation. It was intended to act as the major government instrument to mobilize and channel funds for accelerated development of Ethiopia's agriculture and industry.[10] Since the majority of peasants had too small incomes to spend on agricultural improvements, the Development Bank of Ethiopia did initiate a small agricultural loan program in the 1950s. The benefits went to those who could afford the collateral necessary to guarantee their loans. Those who did not own land could not benefit from the program.[11] Still, the project failed due to high service costs and default rates, and was discontinued by the mid-1960s. The AIDB was established as a specialized credit institution for lending to agriculture. Yet before 1974, no more than 20 percent of agricultural credit was provided by the AIDB and only 25 percent of peasant cropland was treated with fertilizer provided by the government agencies, such as the Agricultural Marketing Corporation.[12]

The World Bank study of Chile, Colombia, Ethiopia, and Honduras indicated that at the time of the survey, larger farmers were the main beneficiaries of institutional credit.[13] Another study revealed that in 1971-1972, only seven percent of the loans granted in this period could be classified as being directed toward those who needed them.[14] Like other financial institutions, AIDB demanded security in land or cash for credit, thus restricting its clientele to the wealthy. The poor and most vulnerable group of farmers was deprived of access to an institutional source of lending. The bank's insistence at lending at commercial rates obviously reduced greatly the number of small farmers who could receive loans. The AIDB also operated as a highly centralized bureaucratic structure, which tended to make it ill suited for lending to large numbers of highly dispersed small farms. Excessive centralization, when dealing with small farmers, often results in increased administrative costs and an inability to adjust programs to local conditions because of political interference.

In order to minimize costs of credit and to enhance credit delivery to the rural community, the use of service cooperatives as intermediary organization between the AIDB and peasants should not be underestimated. In the early years after the Ethiopian revolution, the AIDB channeled short-term loans through service cooperatives to reach small farmers via their peasant associations. On average, about five peasant associations formed a service cooperative. Service cooperatives would be the most appropriate body to implement a savings and credit program in the rural areas of Ethiopia. Another advantage is that service cooperatives have the potential to mobilize resources, including finance and labor, for the development of the peasant sector, and crop marketing and distribution of inputs. Given sufficient freedom and legal support, the service cooperatives would be the most appropriate institution for self-sustaining development in the rural areas of Ethiopia. Sufficient freedom and legal support means less government regulation and interference, as well as legal status and legal protection.

8.3 The Problem of Lending to Small Farmers

It is important to understand why lending to small-scale farmers is so difficult and why they prefer borrowing from informal sources even though rate of interest for such borrowed capital may be higher. Lending institutions refuse loans to poor farmers because they do not have the necessary collateral and are considered "high risk." Financial institutions are discouraged because foreclosure is extremely difficult to implement and often politically unacceptable. Most lending agencies are urban-based and urban-biased. They prefer dealing with industrial and commercial enterprises in urban areas and centers of population. They have rigid procedures for processing loans, whether large or small. Most financial institutions are afraid that there may be failure of farmers to repay their debts on time, or to repay at all. Furthermore, the administrative costs of agricultural credit institutions tend to be higher than most other types of lending institutions. Because borrowers residing in rural areas are widely dispersed, credit distribution, supervision and collection of loans is more costly there than in urban areas.

Nonetheless, modernizing agriculture requires that various kinds of yield-increasing production technology – mechanical, biological, and chemical – be developed and disseminated to farm producers. Examples of such technology are the introduction of new crops species, the adoption of cultivation practices that conserve soil moisture or control pests, new drought or pest-resistant varieties of seeds, chemical pesticides and fertilizers, and improved farm implements or machinery. The question is how to bring together lending institutions and small peasant borrowers in an effort to develop the rural areas of Ethiopia. Most credit agencies require some form of security from farmers, and small farmers have little or no security to offer. Even if lending institutions are willing to grant loans, small-scale farmers are reluctant to borrow money from commercial lending institutions because obtaining and processing documents substantially increases the cost of the loans. These often include the completion of complex forms and a pre-audit of the borrower who, if he is a small farmer, is often illiterate. There are usually delays in processing, and when the funds are finally disbursed the funds and corollary documents can be received only at the office of the lending institution that may be far from the borrower's residence. Moreover, the repayment terms often lack the flexibility to accommodate the natural hazards of farming.

The plight of small Cameroonian farmers, as described by Bouman and Harteveld, is one that applies to other African countries, including Ethiopia:

> Obtaining institutional credit often implies, a day's trip or more to a remote town in unfamiliar surroundings. Institutional credit, particularly where impressive looking banks are involved, carries the aura of aloofness and foreboding. Its splendor, its impersonal approach, its complicated formal and legal procedures rouse the villager's suspicion. The cool, sometimes hostile reception by a condescending clerkdom, makes the ordinary man feel timid and ill at ease. A rotating credit association, however, is home bound. In *djanggi* (an indigenous form of saving and credit in west Cameroon) the villager is amongst his equals in manners and speech. He understands what is going on and is familiar with its mechanism, his rights and obligations.[15]

There is, therefore, great scope for innovation and modification of the rules and regulations that govern the requirements for collateral and the procedures involved for borrowing by small farmers.

8.4 Credit Delivery Methodology

Most credit agencies require some form of security from farmers and small farmers who have little or no security to offer. Such stringent collateral security requirements prevent numerous peasant farmers from participating in credit/savings programs. Since small farmers constitute more than 90 percent of the farming population in Ethiopia, an increased emphasis on small-scale, rather than large-scale, farmers in terms of credit allocation should be encouraged. The best prospect in the future will lie in some form of group responsibility for supervising widely dispersed small farmers such as the Grameen Bank uses in Bangladesh. To avoid loan delinquency and create mutual trust between farmer groups and financial institutions, emphasis should be placed on developing group responsibility. This emphasis on group discipline and financial responsibility should be instilled through constant training and should be strictly enforced.

Instead of concentrating largely in urban centers, lending agencies should open more branches in the rural areas to facilitate the transformation of the rural subsistence sector, as well as promote the banking habit (the use of banks) through the provision of credit and deposit facilities. Rural savings mobilization coupled with deposit-taking activities is a real guarantee for the success of any credit program. In establishing savings/credit programs, considerable emphasis should be placed on training credit program field staff and beneficiaries. Beneficiaries should be given high priority in training that should include "farmer-trains-farmer" methods with content based on group-identified needs. Additional skill training should be organized at national and/or sub-regional level for field staff, taking into account changing program requirements and using appropriate methodologies and teaching aids.

Highly satisfactory repayment rates, exceeding 90 percent, have been reported from the International Fund for Agricultural Development (IFAD), projects in Bangladesh, Benin, Egypt, Malawi, Nepal, Pakistan, Syria, Thailand, Tonga, Turkey and Zambia.[16] These rates are generally well above the recovery rates found in other large-scale small farmer credit programs in Africa which have been about 45-50 percent.[17] The prospects for repayment of loans are greatly enhanced by group responsibility for individual liabilities. Given the cohesiveness of most rural communities when the farmers' association has a stake in an individual performance, it is difficult for the individual member to withstand the pressure of his peers and avoid his obligation.

For the credit program to be effective, however, institutional credit provided to improve production, income, food security and savings of rural households must be complemented by other types of support services, namely, appropriate technical packages, research, extension, training and marketing. In using the group/social collateral approach, smallholder borrowers should be chosen on the basis of established criteria and procedures. Three elements seem important. These are the reputation of the individual within his community, the technical feasibility of the proposed investment in the context of his farm situation, and the expected cash flow that would be generated by the investment.[18] One expert offers some of the best strategies for successful lending and saving mobilization in the rural areas as follows:

> The strategies include a convenient location lending to like-minded individuals and groups of similar economic circumstances, lending based on the borrower's project and reputation rather than on collateral requirements, and the negotiations of loans in the familiar surroundings of potential borrowers, rather than at the desks of bank officers. Also, there are requirements of minimum savings to help develop a savings habit and, as well, the sense of responsibility and repayment morale of borrowers are strengthened by tying lending to savings mobilization.[19]

The key role in this process is played by the development agent who encourages small-scale farmers with similar backgrounds and economic circumstances to come together for informal discussion of their socio-economic situation, the problems they face and the steps they might take to ameliorate their living standards and working conditions. After initiating the process of group discussions and reflection, the development agent attempts progressively to reduce his or her role, leaving it to the villagers themselves to conduct their inquires, form groups and take initiatives to strengthen their economic position. The groups then undertake a variety of income-generating, community and individual activities such as ruminant livestock farming, piggeries, brick-making, and vegetable gardening. Community activities may include construction of water dams, and dikes, anti-erosion works, wells, and afforestation.

Evidence of the successes of financial institutions serving the rural areas can be found. Examples are the innovative approaches undertaken by the Lesotho Agricultural Development Bank, and National Bank of

Kenya under the FAO people's participation projects in Africa. Both of these banks no longer insist on physical collateral to secure a loan. Both emphasize savings first and credit second. Both institutions have demonstrated that the recovery rate for group loans is higher than any other line of credit.

8.5 Informal Savings and Loan Associations

Informal savings and loan associations are vehicles for sustainable development. In many African societies, including Ethiopia, such local financial institutions already exist, some with formal rules and regulations. Savings have proved particularly fertile ground for the emergence of such permanent indigenous structures. Reference was made above in this chapter to the *djanggi*, an indigenous form of savings and credit in West Cameroon. The *harambee* movement in Kenya, the savings clubs in Zimbabwe, and the fixed fund associations in Nigeria are other typical examples of such indigenous institutions.

There are two broad categories of informal financial associations in Ethiopia, *ekub* and *idir*, which could be used for self-reliant development. *Ekub* is a rotating fund. It is an informal savings association of friends, acquaintances, neighbors, office mates, relatives, and peers. *Ekub* members contribute a fixed amount to a fund periodically. These contributions are then allocated to one member at a time in a rotating order. For instance, a group of 15 participants may contribute $5 weekly with total fund of $75 at the end of 15 weeks. After 15 weeks each member would have received $75 when the cycle is completed. The money received would be used for various kinds of investment, e.g., building houses, opening up stores, or purchasing a sewing machine. In some cases, part of the funds may be put into a general fund for productive investment and social services. The purpose of the poor participating in e*kub* is that they are often incapable of otherwise saving enough money in their lifetime to make necessary investments. So they pool their small weekly or monthly savings together, and hand it over to one member on a revolving basis.[20] *Ekub* is also used as a forum for members to discuss economic and social issues.

The other traditional institution that might be helpful for further development of financial institutions is the *idir*. This is the Amharic name for small mutual insurance societies that are almost universal in Ethiopian societies. The *idir* collects funds from its members that are then used to provide some minimal social security, and specially to meet funeral expenses. Members pay the full cost of the funeral, provide food and drinks for the mourners for three days in a row, and provide financial support to the mourning family. The second major function of the *Idir* is to construct schools, roads, health centers, and other social services. Additionally, apart from its role as a financial institution, it may also contribute to the workings of democracy, e.g., promote voting on issues. In the words of an Ethiopian authority on indigenous institutions:

> *Ekub* and *idir*, apart from their central role in economic development activities, may also contribute to democratic working methods through elections of leaders, voting on issues and abiding by the rule of the majority, teaching techniques for running meetings, and introducing the use of bookkeeping and time discipline, etc. In short, they may be a way to integrate modernity into traditional sectors.

Unfortunately, little attention has been paid to the development potential of these local groups. Cooperative development officers have tended to ignore them because they do not normally meet the criteria of the cooperative laws as established in Ethiopia. Yet, where they have been provided with a legal framework of operations, these indigenous self-help groups have served their members well as para-cooperatives and have shown signs of developing as organizations. From the late 1950s, they were used by candidates in parliamentary and municipal council elections as a means of organizing support. In 1966, the government issued a regulation enabling them to be registered. By 1970, there were 395 officially recognized *idir* in Addis Ababa, with 50,723 member households – about one-third of the city's population.[21]

Sources and Notes

[1] Keith Griffin and Roger Hay, "Problems of Agricultural Development in Socialist Ethiopia: An Overview and Suggested Strategy," *Journal of Peasant Studies, Volume 13, No. 1*, (Frank Cass & Co., Ltd., London, 1985), p. 39, 52.

[2] Paul Ojermark, *Planning of Poverty-Oriented Rural Development Projects, Report on the Training Seminar for Field Staff of FAO People's Participation Projects in Africa*, December 2-10, 1985 Mbabane, Swaziland (Food and Agriculture Organization of the United Nations, Rome, 1985), p. 48.

[3] T. W. Oshikoya, "Financial Intermediaries, Resource Mobilization and Agricultural Credit in the Rural Subsistence Sector: The Nigerian Experience," in *Sustainable Agriculture in Africa*, E. Ann McDougall, Editor, (Africa World Press Inc., Trenton, New Jersey, 1987), p. 123, 131.

[4] Paul Ojermark, op. cit., p. 82-83.

[5] Ronald Hope Kempe, Sr., *Development in the Third World: From Policy Failure to Policy Reform*, (M. E. Sharpe, Inc., Armonk, New York and London, 1996) p. 46-48.

[6] T. W. Oshikoya, op. cit., p. 123.

[7] Paul Ojermark, op. cit., p. 36.

[8] A 'usufruct right' is the right to use, but not necessarily the right to own.

[9] Patrick Gilkes, *The Dying Lion, Feudalism and Modernization in Ethiopia*, (Julian Friedmann Publishers Ltd, Show Lane, England, UK, 1975), p. 162.

[10] Ibid., p. 160.

[11] Daniel Teffera, *Economic Development and Nation-Building in Ethiopia*, (Ferris State College, Big Rapids, Michigan, 1986), p. 61.

[12] Edmond J. Keller, *Revolutionary Ethiopia: from Empire to People's Republic*, (Indiana University Press, Bloomington and Indianapolis, 1988), p. 259.

[13] World Bank, *Agricultural Credit: Sector Policy Paper*, (The World Bank, Washington, D.C., May 1975), p. 23.

[14] Patrick Gilkes, op. cit., p. 161.

[15] F. J. A. Bouman and K. Hartevelde quote from *No Shortcuts to Progress: Development Management in Perspective*, Goran Hyden, (University of California Press, Berkeley and Los Angeles, 1983), p. 125.

[16] Mohiuddin Alamgir, "Some Lessons from IFAD's Approach to Rural Poverty Alleviation," Chapter 4 in *Strengthening the Poor: What have we learned?* US-Third World Policy Perspectives, No. 10, Edited by John P. Lewis and Contributors, Overseas Development Council, (Transaction Books, New Brunswick, New Jersey and Oxford, UK, 1988), p. 101.

[17] Paul Ojermark, op. cit., p. 46.

[18] World Bank, op. cit., p. 17-18

[19] Ronald Hope Kempe, Sr., op. cit., p. 48.

[20] Tirfe Mamo, *The Paradox of Africa's Poverty, The role of indigenous knowledge, traditional practices and local institutions: The Case of Ethiopia*, (The Red Sea Press, Trenton, New Jersey, 1999), p. 187.

[21] Ibid., p. 131.

Chapter 9

Participatory Development

9.1 The Concept

In recent years there has been a growing interest in new approaches to national development that bring the poor more rapidly into full *participation* in identifying, designing and implementing solutions to problems of poverty and the environment. The concept of *participation* is variously defined. One of the most inclusive and widely accepted definitions, provided by Bridget Dillon and Matthias Steifel, is that *participation* implies a strengthening of the power of deprived masses of people. Its three main elements are the sharing of power and scarce resources; deliberate efforts by social groups to control their own destinies and improve their living conditions; and the opening up of opportunities from below.[1] The four aspects of *participation* used as a method to alleviate poverty are *participation* in decision-making, *participation* in implementation, *participation* in benefits, and *participation* in evaluation.[2]

Former Tanzanian President Julius Nyerere argued that:

> If people are to be able to develop, they must have power. They must be able to control their own activities within the framework of their village communities. People must participate, not just in the physical labor involved in economic development, but also in the planning of it and the determination of priorities.[3]

Thus it follows that for the *participatory process* to be effective, political and economic power must be held by the people within their communities.

Since democracy is a prerequisite of *participation*, it is assumed here that there is a democratic system of government in place. Democracy requires that important government officials be elected; that those elections be free from fraud; that there be a real possibility of opposition victory; that there be nearly universal citizenship and suffrage; and that civil liberties, including a free mass media and minority rights, be generally respected.[4]

9.2 Obstacles to the Participatory Development Approach

There are still many obstacles to *participation* of the rural poor in development. Most development efforts in poor countries around the world began with what is now generally known as the "top-down" approach, rather than the *participatory* "bottom-up" approach. Governments in many developing countries and international agencies have spent massive amounts of money for development programs in rural areas where the majority of the people, particularly the rural poor, work and live. To a large extent, these efforts have had less impact than desired on improving the lives of the rural populace. Most development projects designed from the "top-down" involved little *participation* of the intended beneficiaries, and seldom provided effective follow-up after projects were completed.[5] Most rural citizens rightfully felt neglected; many became poorer than before because well-intentioned projects were conceived without their involvement and advice.[6] Projects conceived and designed by development agencies and governments based on their view of what should be done with little input from the local people have not usually resolved the constraints to agricultural and rural development. It is very important that local cultures, religious beliefs, felt needs and priorities, indigenous local knowledge, and traditional peasant technologies be taken into account in formulating development programs.

Following recent waves of democratization, many third world countries have successfully implemented the *participatory development process*, but numerous obstacles remain to be addressed in many poor countries, including Ethiopia. The obstacles faced vary from one country to another. In Ethiopia, the greatest impediment during the

Mengistu and present regimes has been the lack of freedom of association and government's heavy-handed involvement in the economy and in the lives of citizens. The removal of independent trade union leaders, the take-over of the Ethiopian teachers associations, the suppression of an independent press, and the expropriation of Gojjam farmers' land to give it to party supporters are typical examples of such obstacles. The peasant associations that were established following the 1974 revolution were at one time considered genuine democratic institutions that would bring about self-reliant and sustainable development in the rural areas of Ethiopia. Unfortunately, the associations became an extension of the state power, rather than agencies for self-administration. Both regimes have regarded collecting taxes and eliminating resistance to change as the two most important functions of the peasant associations, neither of which have received any support from the peasants.[7]

The problem in rural communities of poor countries is the lack of appropriate local organizations and persons with political skills to conduct a broader social revolution. Rural residents must have strong organizations of their own if their voice is to be heard. An organization enhances the power of its members through the aggregation of their individual strengths and through the creation of an organism that can intervene in a coherent and organized fashion to preserve and enhance their interests.

Other obstacles to *participation* are found within the implementing government agencies of each country. The primary problem is that the agencies' centralized nature does not lend itself to encouraging *participation* in decision-making by others. Moreover, these agencies are often located some distance from the rural communities in national or regional capitals, and are out of touch with the rural people they intend to serve.[8] Many governments in poor countries today – beleaguered as they are by external debt, falling prices for their exportable raw materials, and frequently by internal strife – have difficulty engaging in the *participatory development process*. They perceive the *participatory development process* as being too difficult and risky to use. And so it appears easier and safer to stay with a "top-down" development approach.[9]

In fact, rural people have a great deal to contribute to program design. They have a substantial capacity for learning and change, but they also have good reasons to be skeptical of the stranger bearing ideas for improving their lives that are untested in their setting.[10] Building on what the people already know and the resources they already possess has numerous advantages. The adjustments required from them are more easily made, and the risks of employing new methods unsuited to their needs are substantially reduced. Successful programs involve substantial planning with local people, especially in their early stages.[11] Involving the rural people right from the inception, beginning with project identification and planning, is very crucial. Such involvement at an early stage can provide vital information on the local area and prevent misunderstandings as to the nature of the problems and the strategies proposed for their resolution. Among the initial decisions in which local people can be involved are whether the project should start, where it should be located, the way it should be financed and staffed, the path by which they will participate in the project and the contributions they are expected to make. Rural people have their own ideas, beliefs, information, knowledge, technical capabilities and leadership qualities – when they are given the opportunities and are considered participants rather than beneficiaries in joint endeavors to improve their productivity and welfare. Without the active involvement of the people and their organizations in the development process, improvements of human conditions can neither be achieved nor sustained. If planners, administrators and managers acknowledge this basic principle before attempting to implement projects, many resources and much effort could be saved.[12]

9.3 Involving Rural People in Participatory Development

Involving rural people in the planning and implementation of project efforts, as well as in the gains of development, is a necessary condition for self-reliant development. In other words, rural people should take part in the design of agricultural projects at the local level where their knowledge is in some respects greater than that of the change agents. In addition to producing better plans, this approach may also release the latent creative and managerial energy of the rural people. Attention should also be given to the peasant culture, its felt needs, and traditional and existing technologies in order that the information and training packages provided will be in harmony with their rural reality. Furthermore, the solutions must take into consideration the peasants' technical, economic and social capacities, as well as their self-confidence to set about changing their rural reality. In addition to the common people, local religious leaders, schoolteachers, and others who command respect and have easy access to rural families, should be mobilized as part of the project's campaign. They can be instrumental in the bringing about needed attitudinal change.

The most active and enthusiastic sector of any society is the youth. Community organizers should appeal to this group using various creative methods. Introducing events, such as an environmental conservation day in schools and community centers, is an excellent approach to raising awareness. Students and teachers and others interested in the subject should be encouraged to take part in such events. Policy-makers and school administrators should encourage the provision of courses in environmental and sustainable development in their schools.

Non-governmental and other private organizations can significantly contribute towards the production of information, education, and communication materials for teaching the often-illiterate peasants. These teaching/learning materials may cover a wide range of topics, such as soil and water conservation, afforestation, animal rearing, handicraft, and cottage industry. Organizing and conducting workshops for teachers and for those involved in working with the youth can also help increase *participation* and alleviate poverty. Other effective methods include organizing trips for school children to nearby areas to show them the impact of environmental degradation on the community's future ability to survive and grow. The children should be allowed and encouraged to organize events so that they share their experience with their parents and others in the community. These methods of dissemination of information to motivate people in rural communities have proven successful in many parts of the world.

Women are very important to *participatory development* efforts. After the 1974 Ethiopian military revolution, separate organizations for women were created. However, neither before nor after the revolution have women had significant political power in Ethiopia. Although the UN declared 1975 International Women's Year with a major conference held in Mexico City, in Mexico and elsewhere in poor nations, the majority of women are still poor and work extremely hard. For instance, the amount of time spent collecting enough fuel wood for a household's weekly needs varies from 21 hours in Ethiopia to one hour in Nigeria. During that time women carry loads weighing 15 to 35 kilograms as far as ten kilometers.[13] Yet, women remain invisible in statistics because little value is attached to what they do. This is reflected in the less than equal status women hold either in positions of power or in sharing of the community's wealth.

To achieve optimal community *participation* in any environmental, social or economic program, the active involvement of women is paramount. Women constitute half of the population of the community, and, most importantly, women are particularly interested in economic, social and environmental issues that directly affect them. As noted above, the tedious job of collecting firewood and other biomass is a responsibility that is mainly carried out by women. Because of deforestation, women are forced to travel further away from the areas where they live, often spending many hours collecting wood. For genuine development to take place women must be allowed to participate in the development process with all rights and abilities fully available to them. There can be no successful development efforts, no effective poverty alleviation initiative without addressing the needs of women as direct beneficiaries. Furthermore, often it is necessary to focus on the problems of women who are part of cultural minorities and other discrete ethnic populations. An integrated approach is required; gender and ethnic issues should not be brought in as an afterthought.[14]

The "African Charter for Popular Participation in Development" affirms involving the people by calling for an era in which the *participation* and empowerment of the ordinary men and women are the order of the day. In a rare consensus among its framers, the Charter attests that people's *participation* must be at the heart of Africa's development mission and vision. It confirms that authentic development springs from the collective imagination, experience and decisions of the people.[15]

As Julius Nyerere repeatedly stated, for the *participatory process* to be effective, both political and economic power must be held by people within their communities. Ronald Hope Kempe pointed out that experience shows that effective *participation* cannot be commanded by policy-makers, but must instead be induced through the advocacy of projects that offer sufficient incentives to attract the personal resources of time, energy, and freedom of action away from other urgent and competing tasks of the poor.[16]

Recognizing the vital role of *participation in development*, the UN's Economic and Social Council now recommends that governments adopt popular *participation* as a basic policy measure in their national development strategies. Furthermore governments are to encourage the widest possible active *participation* of all individuals and national non-government organizations, such as the trade unions, youth associations, farmers associations, and women's organizations in the development process in setting goals, formulating policies and implementing plans.[17]

Some of the most apparent arguments for *participatory development* are:

- Services can be provided at a lower cost.
- More will be accomplished.
- Participation leads to a sense of responsibility for the project.
- Participation guarantees that a felt need is involved.
- Participation ensures that things are done in the right way.
- It frees population from dependence on professionals.
- It uses indigenous knowledge and expertise.
- It can be a catalyst for further development efforts.[18]

9.4 Grassroots Organizations

Grassroots organizations in recent years have witnessed a growing interest on the part of donors and developing countries in grassroots organizations as an important alternative institutional approach for strengthening the poor. If poor people are to be active and continually involved in economic and political life, a well-organized movement is essential. In order for common people to state their demands and for their voices to be heard, it is essential that they be organized. Organization, in turn, cannot yield anticipated results if the members do not share responsibilities and participate whole-heartedly to fulfill their desired objectives.[19] Organization is the means through which the collective spirit for change acquires a shape and a form. Through organizations, the individual aspirations for a new world become integrated into the wider collective will of society.

Participation by its very nature necessitates the creation of such grassroots organizations. These organizations must be democratic, independent and self-reliant. It is most important that the leadership at all levels remain accountable to the members of such organizations. Grassroots organizations should be given power to tax and spend according to their priorities in pursuit of their well being. For the grassroots organization to fully participate in the productive activities of their national economies, they must have easy access to economic resources and institutions. Community grass-roots organizations are crucial for effective delivery of goods and services, including financial and technical assistance, from government, donor agencies, and cooperating institutions to targeted beneficiaries. Without such organizations, it is difficult to develop a delivery mechanism to channel assistance to the rural people. Unless people have organizations of their own, unless major social and economic groups in the country have a voice and a role in shaping national policies, genuine development will not occur. Civil servants cannot personally ask every peasant to discuss legislation affecting the rural poor. Even in public hearings, individuals representing only themselves rarely have the resources to make effective presentations. So one of the requirements for the promotion of *participation* is making certain that the poor have organizational channels through which to make decisions, maintain communication, mobilize and manage resources and resolve conflicts.[20]

Uma Lele found that successful programs in Africa involved substantial planning with rural people, especially in the early stages in which basic models were developed. She observed the element of popular *participation* to be consistently important, noting the experience of the Special Rural Development Projects in Kenya where neglect of local people's input had an unfavorable effect on project performance. In general, she found that local *participation* might mean involvement in planning, including assessment of local needs.[21] Even if local people did not participate in planning, at a very minimum they should be informed of plans designed for their areas if they were expected to consent and to cooperate in program implementation. Clearly, *participation* in planning and implementation of programs is needed to develop the self-reliance necessary among rural people for accelerated development.[22]

Grassroots organizations have played a pivotal role in poverty reduction among the rural poor in many developing countries. The small farmer development program in Nepal, farmer and irrigation associations in Taiwan, and the *New Community* movement in South Korea have changed the lives of those nations' rural people. In Africa, the rural savings movement in Zimbabwe, the *Harambee* self-help movement in Kenya, the *six-s* program in Burkina Faso, and the e*kub* in Ethiopia have made substantial contributions to the well being of the underprivileged and the powerless through mobilization of savings and channeling funds to micro-enterprises.

9.5 Collaboration between Government and Grassroots Organizations

The primary role of government is to formulate and implement national and regional economic policies and programs that create an environment to facilitate and support local-level activities and initiatives. The function of grassroots organizations is to act as a motivator and demand mobilizer to assure that local people receive services and benefits from government. There are numerous ways in which governments and grassroots organizations can work together in the context of poverty alleviation.

Three modes of collaboration that governments should encourage are:

- Grassroots organizations assisting government programs for poverty alleviation by mobilizing, informing and educating the poor.
- Grassroots organizations being invited to participate in the planning, implementation and evaluation of the government's poverty alleviation programs.
- Government drawing upon the strategy and design of a grassroots initiative to build a national and regional program around it.[23]

Local organizations tend generally to be better than central governments at adapting services to the needs of the poor. Therefore, local peoples' only hope for bettering themselves collectively is to organize into various local non-governmental groups that then may network themselves into a broader populist movement. The absence or declining government presence in rural development activities can provide a unique opportunity for community-based organizations to operate with less intrusion from central authorities. Nonetheless, it should be realized that no other entity can effectively replace the role of government. Without active involvement of government as partner in the process, no local initiative can deliver all the required services, no matter how well it is designed. Major services, in education, health and infrastructure, require huge sums of capital. Governments have a comparative advantage in mobilizing resources on a large scale, and the nationwide development and diffusion of new farming technologies. Governments have a special responsibility to assist in strengthening and building the capacity of grassroots institutions so they can assume increasing responsibility in managing and implementing project activities with a high degree of autonomy and self-reliance. Governments and grassroots organizations have differing, but complementary strengths. Therefore government and local organizations should work together as partners in development. This partnership requires government accountability, transparency and honest governance.[24]

Also grassroots organizations should work with private business, religious groups, line ministries, cooperating institutions, and other development agencies at the local level. Thus they should be able to establish horizontal and vertical linkages so as to avoid dependency on one entity. Grassroots organizations should be seen as vehicles for economic progress, social emancipation and political empowerment of the poor.

9.6 The Ethiopian Experience with Grassroots Organizations

Norman Uphoff was correct in stating that local organizations should reach beyond the grassroots level through a federation of local-level organizations.[25] A good example of this has been the Ethiopian Peasant Associations. These grassroots organizations elected their representatives to district farmers' associations and these in turn elected representatives to regional associations. Regional associations elected representatives to the provincial farmers' associations. In turn, the members of the provincial farmers' associations elected their representatives to the national association.

TABLE 9
ORGANIZATIONAL STRUCTURE OF PEASANT ASSOCIATIONS
FROM VILLAGE TO NATIONAL LEVEL

Kebele-level Peasant Associations (KPA's)	23,500
Woreda-level Peasant Associations (WPA's)	571
Awraja-level Peasant Associations (APA's)	102
Provincial-level Peasant Associations (PAS's)	14
All-Ethiopia Peasant Association (AEPA)	1

Source: *The Paradox of Africa's Poverty, The role of indigenous knowledge, traditional practices and local institutions: The Case of Ethiopia*, by Terfe Mamo, (The Red Sea Press, 1999), p. 120.

We have touched above upon how these farmers associations were involved in rural development activities following the military revolution in 1974. It was intended that the All-Ethiopian Peasant Association would coordinate and control the activities of the Peasant Associations. The Ethiopian Peasant Association is an example of a national grassroots organization whose development aspirations were stifled. It was argued above that for effective *participation* of the people in development efforts there must be an organization of the rural poor that they call their own. The overwhelming majority of the world's poor live in villages. They do not *participate* effectively in the development of their countries because they lack such institutions at the grassroots level. Setting up grassroots organizations as described above is a matter of priority for rural development if such institutions are not in existence.

Following the 1975 Land Reform Proclamation, community-based and grassroots organizations such as peasant associations, farmer associations, women, and youth associations were established throughout Ethiopia. The Peasant Associations had multiple roles and performed varied functions. For instance, Peasant Associations assumed a wide range of responsibilities, including implementation of government land-use directives; adjudication of land disputes; encouragement of development programs, such as water and land conservation; construction of schools and clinics; organizing forestry programs; and road construction. The Peasant Associations, as noted above, had ascending layers with representatives chosen from lower-level entities up to the national level.

Although the Mengistu regime granted the Peasant Associations broad functions and responsibilities, their *participation* in decision-making above the level of the individual local association was minimal. Similarly, the resources needed to exercise power effectively were missing. In spite of the fact that the Peasant Associations undertook many positive steps, their role in development was very limited. The Peasant Associations functioned much like an agency of the government, disseminating information and directives of the government to lower levels of administration. As the central government sought to impose its policies on the countryside through the local associations, the associations' leaders lost enthusiasm and legitimacy in the process that required them to transmit these policies to their members.

As Christopher Clapham observed, the peasants' main objective of promoting rural projects received no support from officials of the government.[26] The Peasant Associations became instruments for transmission of official directives rather than institutions through which members' interests and concerns were articulated to government. Through the Peasant Associations, the local people demanded more *participation* than the government was willing to allow. Therefore, many of the goal-oriented and conscientious Peasant Association leaders were replaced by political cadres. Realizing the pivotal position of the peasants' organizations, the military government created parallel alternative parastatal organizations, thereby paralyzing the peasants' potential power.

Nonetheless, even today the Ethiopian Peasant Associations offer promising possibilities to play a major role in efforts to eradicate rural poverty. The institutional foundations of the Peasant Associations have already been created, and they have demonstrated the capacity to mobilize local people for various causes and for community activities. To be effective development grassroots entities, the Peasant Associations must be autonomous and free from government pressure and interference. Any future government involvement in the affairs of local-level organizations should consciously be limited and carefully fused with the efforts of the local people.[27]

The All-Ethiopia Peasants Association might play a catalytic role in facilitating *participation* by all social groups from the grassroots to the national chamber of commerce in the development process. Also the All-Ethiopia Peasants Association could lobby and continue to put pressure on the government to meet its responsibilities of providing essential services, and to institute needed land reform policies and measures to help relieve population pressure on the land. Change agents would be needed to train and assist local Peasant Association members in finding solutions to felt needs using available resources, and in identifying resources that are beyond the means of communities.[28]

9.7 A Methodology for Promotion of Participatory Development

Following the 1979 World Conference on Agrarian Reform and Rural Development (WACARRD), the Food and Agricultural Organization (FAO) took a leading role in promoting *people's participation in rural development* through promotion of self-help organizations in developing countries. The FAO projects focused on the rural and the urban poor, male and female. Concerned with the lack of institutional credit available to the majority of small farmers in developing countries, FAO established a "guarantee-cum risk fund" (GCRF) with collaborating banking institutions to serve as an ultimate guarantee in case of loan default, and as an incentive for the bank to provide a credit line to target groups.[29] In this process, before an application for credit was approved, the pre-project situation of the area was determined through socio-economic investigation of the village concerned by a group organizer. The group organizer was a catalytic agent of the implementing agency and key to the success of the *participatory* projects. The targeted beneficiaries were then encouraged to come together for discussion among themselves and with development workers. Out of this process, groups of nine to twelve members each emerged to form the basic units around which a credit program was organized.

Since 1982, the FAO has embarked upon a number of *people's participation projects* in Africa, one of which was the Chekalini Irrigation Project in Western Kenya. This author had the privilege to represent FAO and participate in that project from its inception. The *people's participation project* refocused attention on one of the poorest parts of the country, the Kakamega District in Western Kenya. Popular participation in the Chekalini Irrigation Project was promoted using a group savings/credit program. The project started with only eight settlers, migrants from the former White Highlands of Kenya, who farmed in the Chekalini farm settlement scheme near Kakamega town. This was a dry farming settlement area, remote from government services, ethnically diverse, but with settlers committed to self-reliant development.

Maize production was the principal occupation, but income from this activity was low and alternative employment opportunities for women were not available. The group undertook a variety of income-generating activities, such as horticulture and vegetable gardening by irrigation, in addition to staple crop and stock farming. Their farm produce was marketed for the fast-growing population of Kakamega town. The basic objectives of the projects were to increase the incomes and standard of living of the settler community and to promote *participation* and self-reliance within the Chekalini farm settlement scheme. The settlers had not received funds or technical services to raise local production, nor was local *participation in development* encouraged until the FAO project was initiated in 1983. The settlers were organized into a small self-sustaining group with the assistance of a group promoter to receive credit for individual and joint activities. The concept of "saving first" and "credit second" was emphasized to first demonstrate that a regular voluntary savings habit was a prerequisite to loan eligibility. The savings/credit component commenced in 1984. Following an agreement between FAO and the National Bank of Kenya for the establishment of the GCRF, FAO deposited US$30-40,000 in National Bank of Kenya. Then the settlers were provided with credit on a group-guarantee basis without additional collateral. The loans were modest in size and of short duration. The principal was repaid in weekly installments over a twelve-month period. Weekly meetings were held for members to evaluate progress, identify new problems, initiate new studies, and pay their weekly contributions to the group savings. The economic capacity of the members was enhanced by the provision of training courses in a wide range of skills such as brick making, grain-storage, dairying, and simple book keeping.

By 1985, project beneficiaries had already elected a loan committee to replace project staff in managing the credit/saving activities, giving them more independence from outside agencies. The linkage of savings and credit services to small farmers within a single institution was one of the success stories of this program. Another important achievement was the acceptance of lending institutions to use social collateral in lieu of physical collateral. This had been the greatest impediment for small farmers to access institutional lending.

These small farmers demonstrated their ability, not only to pay high rates of interest, but also to repay both principal and interest in a timely manner. The recovery rate for their loans was 98 percent, among the highest in the world. After seeing that the project was viable, nearby farmers expressed their desire to join the project. As of March 1985, its membership had increased from ten to 220 farmers, organized in fourteen mixed and six female groups. Seasonal loans disbursed in 1985 amounted to more than 500,000 Kenyan shillings (US$31,250), while group savings mobilized totaled approximately 60,000 Kenyan shillings (US$3,750). Rural savings mobilization was relatively new in Kenya and for that matter in Africa, but project beneficiaries demonstrated their willingness to save. This is contrary to the common belief that the rural poor cannot save because they are poor. Given the meager income of subsistence farmers, and the fact that the project was only one year old, the amount of mobilized savings was particularly noteworthy. A 1984 evaluation pointed out the need to encourage group formation so that the poorest residents, particularly women, were empowered to seek additional resources. At that time, a pre-existing irrigation project with financial and technical assistance was integrated into an expanded project to organize more homogeneous groups and activities in surrounding villages.

Similar success stories are to be found across the continent in countries such as Ghana, Swaziland and Lesotho where saving/credit schemes have become the principal vehicle for promoting people's *participation* in development efforts. Because these pilot programs have been successful, some African states have already started to replicate the pilot projects over wider areas of their countries. The positive results of such *participatory development* activities are due to the major role of targeted beneficiaries in decision-making, as well as the utilization of local knowledge and experience in planning, implementing and evaluating day-to-day activities. Another reason has been accessibility to institutional credit based on the group-guarantee concept.

Sources and Notes

[1] See Dharam Ghai, *Participatory Development: Some Perspectives from Grass-Roots Experience*, A paper contributed to the International Conference on Popular Participation in the Recovery and Development Process in Africa, 12-16 February 1990, (Economic Commission for Africa/United Nations, Arusha, United Republic of Tanzania, 1990), p. 3-4. "Participation" was initially emphasized worldwide in the 1950s in community development (CD) and in the 1970s in integrated rural development (IRD) programs. For more on these efforts, see Lane E. Holdcroft, "The Rise and Fall of Community Development, 1950-65: A Critical Assessment," Chapter 3 in *Agricultural Development in the Third World*, Carl K. Eicher and John M. Staatz, Editors, (The Johns Hopkins University Press, Baltimore and London, 1984), p. 46-58, and *Rural Development Today: A Practical Perspective*, Agricultural Economics Report, No. 315, (Michigan State University, East Lansing, Michigan, January 1977).

[2] John M. Cohen and Norman T. Uphoff, "Participation's Place in Rural Development: Seeking Clarity through Specificity," (*World Development, Volume 8*, Pergamon Press Ltd, Great Britain, 1980), p. 219.

[3] Quoted in Ronald Hope Kempe, Sr., *Development in the Third World: From Policy Failure to Policy Reform*, (M.E. Sharpe, Inc., Armonk, New York and London, 1996), p. 104.

[4] Howard Handelman, *The Challenge of Third World Development*, (Prentice Hall, Upper Saddle River, New Jersey, 1996), p. 247.

[5] David C Korten, "Community Organization and Rural Development: A Learning Process Approach," (*Public Administration Review, Volume 40*, September/October 1980), p. 491.

[6] Stephen K. Ameyaw, "Rural Development Perspective: Conducting Policy and Constraints on Practice," in *Sustainable Agriculture in Africa*, edited by E. Ann McDougall, (Africa World Press Inc., Trenton, New Jersey, 1990), p. 90.

[7] Christopher Clapham, *Transformation and Continuity in Revolutionary Ethiopia*, (Cambridge University Press, Cambridge, New York, New Rochelle, Melbourne, Sydney, 1988), p. 160.

[8] Ronald Hope Kempe, Sr, op. cit., p. 105.

[9] FAO, *Development Support Communication, FAO Expert Consultation Report, 8-12 June 1987* (Food and Agricultural Organization, Rome, Italy, 1987), p. 19.

[10] David C. Korten, op. cit., p. 498.

[11] John M. Cohen and Norman T. Uphoff, op. cit., p. 220.

[12] Ibid., p. 213.

[13] Liz Osborn, "Women and Trees: Indigenous Relations and Agro-Forestry Development," in *Sustainable Agriculture in Africa,* edited by E. Ann McDougall, (Africa World Press Inc., Trenton, New Jersey, 1990), p.138.

[14] Mohiuddin Alamgir, "Some lessons from IFAD's Approach to Rural Poverty Alleviation," in *Strengthening the Poor: What Have We Learned?* U.S. Third World Policy Perspectives, No. 10, edited by John P. Lewis and Contributors, (Overseas Development Council, Transaction Books, New Brunswick and Oxford, 1988), p. 33.

[15] UN/ECA, *Communication for Participatory Development: A Training Manual,* (United Nations Economic Commission For Africa, Addis Ababa, Ethiopia, 1994), p. iii.

[16] Ronald Hope Kempe, Sr, op. cit., p. 105-106.

[17] John M. Cohen and Norman T. Uphoff, op. cit., p. 213.

[18] Ben Wisner, *Power and Need in Africa,* (Africa World Press Inc., Trenton, New Jersey, 1989), p. 268.

[19] Tirfe Mammo, *The Paradox of Africa's Poverty, The role of indigenous knowledge, traditional practices and local institutions: The Case of Ethiopia,* (The Red Sea Press, Inc, 1999), p. 223.

[20] David C. Korten, op. cit., p. 499.

[21] Uma Lele, *The Design of Rural Development: Lessons from Africa,* (Johns Hopkins Press, Baltimore, 1975), p. 150.

[22] Samuel Paul, "Assisted Self-Reliance: Working with, Rather Than for, the Poor" in *Strengthening the Poor: What Have We Learned? U.S. Third World Policy Perspectives, No.10,* edited by John P. Lewis and Contributors, (Overseas Development Council, Transaction Books, New Brunswick and Oxford, 1988), p. 33.

[23] Ibid., p. 28-29.

[24] UN/ECA, *Poverty Alleviation and Environmental Conservation: A Training Manual, Number 4,* (United Nations Economic Commission for Africa, Addis Ababa, Ethiopia, 1994), p. 3.

[25] John M. Cohen and Norman T. Uphoff, op. cit., p. 54.

[26] Christopher Clapham, op. cit., p. 160-161.

[27] Fassil B. Kiros, *The Subsistence Crisis in Africa: The Case of Ethiopia,* (Organization for Social Sciences Research in Eastern Africa, Nairobi, Kenya, 1993), p. 200.

[28] UN/ECA, op. cit., p. 3.

[29] FAO, *Planning of Poverty-Oriented Rural Development Projects, Report on the Training Seminar for Field Staff of FAO People's Participation Projects in Africa,* 2-10 December 1985, Mbabane, Swaziland (Food and Agriculture Organization of the United Nations, Rome, 1985), p. 78.

Chapter 10

Development Support Communication

In this term, the word *Development* is first and *Support Communication* follows, indicating *communication that supports development.* Communication is better described than defined. It is relatively new as a separate field of study although Aristotle and other ancient philosophers pondered how meaning became attached to words and symbols, and how it was shared through human inter-actional processes.[1]

Development Support Communication is defined in a number of ways. A pioneer on this subject, Nora Quebral, offers the following:

> Development Communication is the art and science of human communication applied to the speedy transformation of a country and the mass of its people to a dynamic state of economic growth that makes possible greater social equality and the larger fulfillment of the human potential.[2]

Others define it as the sharing of knowledge aimed at reaching a consensus for action that takes into account the interests, needs, and capacities of all concerned.[3] Sharing is not a one-way transfer of information; it implies rather an exchange between communication equals. When communication takes place, on the one hand, change agents who are technical specialists learn about rural people's felt needs, aspirations, and their techniques of production; on the other, the people learn of the techniques and proposals of the change agents.[4]

The problem hitherto has been that useful sharing of knowledge often has not taken place spontaneously between change agents and rural people because neither side has acquired the necessary skills to overcome certain barriers. Foremost among these barriers have been socio-cultural ones; development efforts have been often undermined by incompatible communication approaches, by a clash of differing levels of education and literacy, and by differing use of language. The ultimate purpose of knowledge-sharing should be to empower rural people to take increasing control over their environment – their agriculture, health, habitat, and other factors that so critically impinge upon their quality of life.[5]

Wood and Gecolea describe *Development Support Communication* as one of the tools that rural development program managers should use in planning and implementing their programs. It is a *support tool* particularly for helping strengthen the *service delivery capabilities of programs at the village level*. This is achieved in practice through using communication resources to support: preparation of reference and teaching materials; educational aids to help change agents be more effective communicators; mass media activities that are closely coordinated with the change agent's programs; and management information systems for program evaluation and monitoring.[6]

A well-known theory articulated by Laswell defined communication as, "who says what in which channel to whom with what effect."[7] From this and similar theories, communication was originally seen as a straight linear process whereby information was sent from a source over some channel to a receiver who was affected by the message. The *Sender-Message-Receiver* model is one such model of this process.

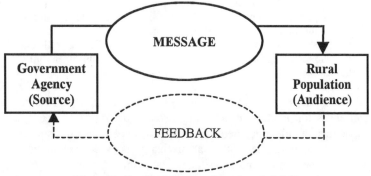

Figure 1. Sender-Message-Receiver Model

The *Sender-Message-Receiver* model gives the notion of the message coming from a government source and being received at the village level by the rural people, without any feedback. Feedback is the response, intended or spontaneous, that the target audience (rural people) sends after receiving the message. Without *feedback*, it is a "top-down" process with only a one-way information flow from government agencies to the rural population. This model presents the audience as rather passive, which is not and should not be the case, and usually it does not work.

The *Source-Message-Audience-Feedback* model has been proven more effective in communicating with rural people.

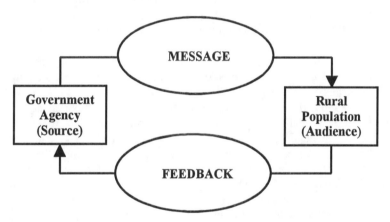

Figure 2. Source-Message-Audience-Feedback Model

In this model, the *source* is the change agent. The content of his or her message provides the motivation for change. The *message* is sent through one or more communication channels to an *audience* of rural people. The channel may be the change agent speaking directly to the *audience*, or the channel may be in the form of a poster, or a result or method demonstration. Sometimes drama, songs, and dances are appropriate. The above may be presented directly to a live audience, or via the mass media channels of newspapers, radio, or television. Both the change agent *source* and members of the rural *audience* should alternate as senders and receivers of messages. *Feedback* is the flow of messages, intended or spontaneous, from the *audience* back to the *source*. *Feedback* encourages active community participation. It is the key to successful implementation of rural programs. Without *feedback*, we cannot determine whether we have communicated effectively or not.

10.1 Development Support Communication in Rural Development

It has been almost three decades since *Development Support Communication* began to be used by the United Nations. The first such effort, the Development Training and Communication Planning Project (DTCPP), was launched in the late 1960s for the Asia and the Pacific region jointly by the United Nations Development Program (UNDP) and the United Nations Children Fund (UNICEF). The goal of the DTCPP was to help governments in the region build capabilities to address two common constraints in rural development programs. These were the lack of effective training to develop human resources, and poor utilization of information and communication methods and materials.[8]

In 1969, the UNDP circulated a request to UN member agencies to the effect that attention be given to communication inputs for development aid projects. As a consequence, all of the UN member agencies started to promote some particularly innovative and interesting experimental activities in *Development Support Communication*. The United Nations Educational, Scientific, and Cultural Organization (UNESCO) concentrated its attention on the mass media, including the promotion of local newspapers and radio stations to serve rural communities. The United Nations Family and Population Agency (UNFPA) had always employed communication in its family planning educational programs. The Food and Agricultural Organization (FAO), the World Health Organization (WHO), and other UN agencies involved in agriculture, primary health care, and community development extension services had long employed printed materials and audio-visual teaching aids to supplement the interpersonal communication between their hard-pressed, frequently ill-equipped, field staff and rural people.[9]

The subject matter areas of information, education, and communication continued to gain momentum during the 1970s, and the Joint United Nations Information Committee recommended in 1980 that special efforts be made to, "promote the inclusion of an information component in every development project in the UN system." Subsequently, the Administrative Coordinating Council endorsed in 1982 this general recommendation and confirmed the vital role that communication support can provide in development activities.[10]

The 1979 FAO-sponsored World Conference on Agrarian Reform and Rural Development reinforced the mandate for communication in support of rural development. It placed special emphasis on participation of the rural poor; not simply in sharing the benefits of development, but also in sharing the responsibility for development decision-making. The Conference concluded that:

> Rural development strategies can realize their full potentials only through the motivation, active involvement and organization at the grassroots level of rural people, with special emphasis on the least advantaged in conceptualizing and designing policies and programs, and in creating administrative, social and economic institutions, including cooperatives and other voluntary forms of organizations, for complementing and evaluating them.

There was widespread agreement that to be successful, development strategies must engender understanding and awareness of the problems and opportunities of rural people at all levels, and improve the interaction between development personnel and rural people through efficient communication systems. This meant that no development strategy was complete unless communication policies and activities were incorporated in the design and implementation of program priorities.[11]

As indicated above, the critical role of *Development Support Communication* in human development and poverty alleviation through active participation and empowerment of beneficiaries has been amply demonstrated in United Nations and other aid agency-supported programs. Its role in informing and motivating intended beneficiaries, promoting their increased participation in development at all levels, and providing training to rural change agents, rural producers and other relevant groups, has become much better understood among development practitioners.

Unfortunately, the formulation and use of effective communication strategies have been left out of most sub-Saharan African development programs. There are at least two reasons for this. Some African governments do not understand the strategic role of *Development Support Communication* or how to incorporate it into development projects. Secondly, although sub-Saharan Africa is the most underdeveloped region in the world, no donor or host country agency has been willing to finance an African development training and communication-planning program, similar to that established in Asia over three decades ago. While there are a few modest communication-training centers in North Africa, there are virtually none in sub-Saharan Africa. Part of the problem is that technology issues have continued to dominate development thinking, often with concomitant neglect of issues of human behavioral change required in the development process.

10.2 Development Support Communication Activities

The main kinds of *Development Support Communication* activities proven effective in supporting successful agricultural and rural development programs are:

- Production of video films, radio programs, newspaper articles, audio tape recordings, posters, flip charts, leaflets, pamphlets, and bulletins that complement and support change agents' efforts in rural areas.
- Deployment of video shows, radio broadcasts, news articles, printed materials including posters, to reinforce extension messages.
- Enhancement of the communication skills and technical capabilities of change agents by conducting pre-service and in-service training programs.
- Production of suitable media materials for communication in the rural environment for educational, informational and extension communication purposes directed at various target groups such as change agents, small-scale farmers, small-enterprise owners, women's groups, and the general public.
- Training of administrators of development programs, media managers, educational personnel, public relations officers, trainers, project managers, planners, and rural community leaders in communication concepts and skills. These concepts and skills result in more effective communicators, and generally improved information flows at all levels and in all directions. This means promoting horizontal communication (from planners to planners, technicians to technicians, groups of people to groups of people), and by vertical communication (from planners to grassroots-level

intended beneficiaries and feedback from the grassroots-level to planners).

- Assessment of the communication needs and existing networks of the community and its opinion leaders so as to clarify, strengthen, and improve the two-way communication channels between the change agents and intended beneficiaries to enhance community participation, empowerment, problem-solving and decision-making exercises, training, and institution-building activities.

- Assisting the intended beneficiaries in prioritizing problems that affect their socio-economic well being and productive capacity, in finding relevant information for consideration of such concerns, and directing messages to relevant public and private entities for common understanding and possible action.

- Assisting the intended beneficiaries in developing their communities' capacities for solving issues on their own and in collaboration with others.

10.3 Transfer of Technology vis-a-vis Knowledge Utilization

Developing countries and international agencies have spent incredible amounts of money for development programs in the rural areas where the majority of the rural poor reside and work. Many of these efforts have not been successful in improving the well being of the intended beneficiaries – the smallholder farm families, sharecroppers, the landless, artisans, and other disadvantaged rural people who make up a large proportion of the rural population.

Numerous studies in Asia and Latin America have shown that there has been an over-reliance on the so-called "transfer of technology" to bring about development, rather than adequately focusing on more effective knowledge utilization by the intended beneficiaries. The assumption was that researchers would determine the composition of the improved information and technology, the "technology package," and that it only had to be passed on to the farmer for development to take place. This approach focused on increased productivity alone, with little attention given to understanding and ascertaining the needs and aspirations of those people who would be affected by the new technology. It was assumed wrongly that automatically there would be desired attitudinal and behavioral changes among the rural people. Little or no thought was given as to whether the technology being provided was suited to the beneficiaries' needs as they perceived them, and to their possibilities of assimilating them.

From both research and experience, leaders in rural development efforts increasingly realize that creating new technologies and disseminating information on new technologies to rural people does not automatically mean that the intended beneficiaries will accept them. Often well-designed programs and attractive technologies fail to produce the intended changes in behavior and attitudes of the targeted rural people. A number of questions can be asked in this regard. Is the technology advocated by the rural development program relevant to the needs of the intended beneficiaries? Is it in forms that the beneficiaries can use? What factors hinder the villagers from using the knowledge? And how can program planners and managers overcome problems related to knowledge utilization in order to achieve the social transformation being sought? The solutions have to take into consideration the beneficiaries' capacities in every sense – technical, economic, social, and psychological – if there are to be changes in their reality.

Therefore, the emphasis today must be, not only on the generation of new technology, but also on how such technology is to be disseminated and utilized. This approach involves additional change agent training, in addition to communication and media materials and equipment support. The ultimate goal of most rural-based development programs at the village level is to motivate farmers to change current inefficient or bad practices by getting them to participate in decision-making on issues affecting their lives. This is the current challenge for all those involved in rural development programs. The traditional communication approach has been to tell the people what they had to do. This almost never works. Too often the villagers are blamed for their unwillingness to participate because of ignorance and traditional beliefs. Development agency staff needs to listen to the villagers and learn why they are not participating and then modify development programs to address the villagers' real needs.

Effective use of audio-visual aids, and traditional and mass media, in addition to inter-personal contact, can enhance the widespread acceptance of information. Such strategies should be an integral part of the design and implementation of development projects. The goal of many programs is to introduce technology such as high yielding crop varieties to enhance income, high protein diets to improve health, and improved farm implements to discourage slash and burn techniques. The goal of the farmers, however, may be spreading risk and labor resources more effectively, producing grains that store better and are less prone to disease, or have a superior taste. This means that one major component of the development process must focus on the understanding of change agents about farmer participation in the program. Research supports the hypothesis that the most successful rural programs are those in which the intended beneficiaries themselves have participated in program conception and planning. Rural people must become its prime movers, not its passive beneficiaries.

10.4 Needs Assessment and Audience Analysis

Program designers and change agents must understand the rural audience to be effective in communication and in planning village-level rural programs. *Needs assessment* and *target audience analysis* are two techniques, both useful in learning about a target audience.

Needs assessment is the process of identifying development needs by gathering relevant information and assessing the villagers' perceived needs, interests, ambitions, constraints, requirements and priorities in a given community; and then addressing these in planning a community-specific program. This may require community and household surveys and special studies, building on relevant existing records and reports.

Target audience analysis refers to searching existing documentation, and conducting baseline surveys of knowledge, attitudes, and communication practices. Its aim is to understand the beliefs, attitudes, values, problems, behavioral patterns, local communication systems, and media habits of the community. *Target audience analysis* entails knowing who the target audiences are, what their communications needs are, and how it defines them. Research has shown that mere provision of information does not guarantee acceptance or adoption of innovation. Through *target audience analysis* it is possible to determine those factors that may hinder or help adoption of new innovations.

Once the current social, cultural and psychological factors within a community are identified, ways of addressing them that would allow a free and effective flow of information can be found. Through *target audience analysis*, program designers and implementers can find out how beneficiaries would be involved and participate in a program from the beginning. Participation of the target audience is crucial because it brings about some degree of commitment needed if the program is to be sustainable. Also, understanding the audience leads to preparation of messages and selection of communication channels that are appropriate for the audience. In order to maximize their impact, most programs now recommend the use of multiple channels of communication with reinforcing messages orchestrated in pre-determined sequences.[12]

In affluent societies, such as Western Europe and North America, a wide range of media is available from which to select and pass messages to a specific target group. In many developing countries, Ethiopia included, the majority of rural people are illiterate. They can not read and write. Effective communication with such people is difficult. Using modern communications media, such as television, is especially costly and may be used only in urban areas where electricity is available. Newspapers, magazines, and other print materials are expensive and require literate audiences. Communicators must know which combination of channels would give the best results. Not all media are credible or accessible to the target audience. It is therefore necessary to find out through *target audience analysis* which media or other channels the audience has access to, which media or other channels they trust, and which they prefer for whatever reason. Failure to do this could mean using media or other channels that the audience does not have access to or does not trust.

While there is no proven formula in selecting media or other channels for agricultural and rural development, certain guidelines have emerged from practice. We know for example that radio is good at reaching a lot of people quickly with simple messages; print media such as posters and pamphlets are good reminders or re-enforcers of radio broadcasts; and interpersonal sources are most useful for attitudinal evolution and adding credibility to media content. Small media combinations are also very effective at the grassroots level. The change agent's use of video combined with simple, well-illustrated pamphlets has proven to be an excellent channel mix for direct training of farmers and rural people.

Communication as practiced today does not rely only on media – interpersonal and traditional channels such as songs, dances, oral literature, music, also play an important role. These forms of media are effective and are highly regarded as appropriate for use in Ethiopian traditional areas because they are community-owned and therefore rural people easily identify with them. Also these media require little equipment or materials and are basically free of cost.

Successful *Development Support Communication* strategies documented around the world have been based on a mix of media, planned in a systematic way. Often they have used audience segmentation, i.e., have categorized rural people into groups rather than considering them as a homogeneous mass. For example, people of different ages, gender, and literacy levels may have different information needs, as may people of different social and economic status. Therefore, often these groups must be targeted separately.

Program designers and change agents who use *needs assessment* and *target audience analysis* will have a better understanding of the issues that concern the community. They will also understand how to handle these issues and how best to communicate them to various target audiences.

10.5 Target Groups in Ethiopia

The ultimate beneficiaries of *Development Support Communication* are the rural populace, and disadvantaged and marginalized urban and peri-urban population groups of Ethiopia. They comprise more than 80 per cent of the nation's population. The rural population is engaged in agricultural production and must produce food to feed the country. The use of *Development Support Communication* in rural programs could help slow the drift of young, under and unemployed people to urban areas by contributing to increased productivity and making farming more rewarding. The urban poor would also benefit from increased food production and therefore increased food availability at lower prices. Both rural and urban poor would benefit from using *Development Support Communication* to strengthen health and nutrition, housing and urban development, income generation, and social services programs. Over the long-term, there would be changes in the knowledge, attitude, values, and practices of communities, development workers, administrators, and policy-makers with more effective use of *Development Support Communication*. This would eventually improve the quality of life of the population at large in Ethiopia, as has been evidenced in Asia and Latin America.

In Ethiopia, with its limited electronic mass media, the extension worker has been the main link for scientific improvement in agriculture between the researcher and the farmer. Extension workers coped as best they could, but were too few and spread too thinly in relation to the number of farmers requiring information and training. Transportation difficulties also limited their reach. The dearth of rural extension services seriously hampered the capability of rural communities to receive needed information related to improved agricultural technologies. Until recently, very few Ethiopians had ever talked to an extension worker in agriculture, forestry, health, nutrition, family planning, environmental or women's programs, home economics or area development. Very few had ever seen a film or poster, read a newsletter, or listened to educational radio programs.

To its credit, the current Ethiopian government has made a major commitment to expanding agricultural extension services in rural Ethiopia. Its New Extension Program builds on the success of the Ministry of Agriculture/Sasakawa-Global 2000 pilot program started in 1993. After two years of pilot program experience with its focus on introducing new technologies, the Ministry launched and rapidly expanded the New Extension Program with its focus on increasing total national production. The number of trained extension workers increased five-fold to 15,000 in 1994, and some three million farmers' plots were using improved technologies by 1998. As might be expected, there are problems associated with the rapidly expanding program. However, these problems, including quality of extension workers, and amount of production credit, improved seed and fertilizer available, are being addressed.[13]

The farmer must have access to production credit, and improved seeds, fertilizer, and herbicides at reasonable prices. They do know about the advantages of improved seeds and the application of fertilizer and herbicides, and they want to use the improved technologies. The reason for the failure of the technologies to diffuse has little to do with the farmers' attitude as is commonly claimed. Rather it is that the inputs often are not available.[14] The Ethiopian government and private sector generally have been unable to provide adequate amounts or varieties of improved seeds to stimulate and meet farmer demand for these inputs. In 1995/96, it is estimated that only 28 percent of Ethiopian farmers used inorganic fertilizer and three percent used improved seed. Peasant farmers would use these inputs if they were readily available and reasonably priced. Inadequate production and distribution of high-yielding varieties of quality seed have become one of the major constraints in increasing food crop production in Ethiopia. For the 1995-96 cropping season, selected improved cereal seeds were supplied to farmers as part of the New Extension Program "technology package" in Harar. However, the supply and utilization of improved seed provided only eight percent of farmer demand. Clearly there is the need for more private or cooperative seed growers that could guarantee the availability of seeds in a timely manner.[15]

Three principal problems are evidenced in the New Extension program. First, there are now too many farm families per extension worker. Second, too many non-extension tasks are being imposed on extension agents. These include, but are not limited to, processing credit applications, loan collection, and distribution of fertilizer and other inputs. The third and most difficult problem is that the EPRDF government has been encouraging and supporting EPRDF-affiliated businesses and EPRDF-affiliated NGO's to provide inputs – while harassing and discouraging the more efficient private sector firms and other NGO's from such activities. The Front-affiliated entities perform poorly, but continue to be favored because of their ties to the Front. The EPRDF theorists fear that these "lower members of the intelligentsia" would undermine the Front's influence and development programs if they oppose the party's political line. The theorists are concerned that the counter-propaganda of representatives of government organizations and NGO's might persuade peasants to deny support to the EPRDF and obstruct the hegemony of revolutionary democracy. Therefore a EPRDF strategy document concludes, "The government organizations and NGO's development workers must be brought over to the side of the Front." [16] It has become a common practice for the EPRDF government to threaten international NGO's with expulsion. There are now some 250 NGO's working in Ethiopia to fight hunger and poverty. The EPRDF government is concerned that some NGO's could expose unfair government practices in the rural areas. It may be recalled that some NGO's were instrumental in exposing the *Derg's* abusive food policies of the 1980s.

Although *Development Support Communication* would not address the availability of production inputs, it could help improve the quality of extension workers and the overall effectiveness of the New Extension Program. The use of radio and a variety of audio-visuals, along with interpersonal contact and communication would be particularly effective.

Even with the recent attention given to reaching rural producers, only about one-third of Ethiopia's nine million farm families have benefited from the New Extension Program to date. The plan to deploy one trained extension worker per 800 farm families, although an improvement over the past, is inadequate. Even if the ratio were adequate, the financial resources required to recruit, train, and maintain the large field staff needed to cover the entire country would not be available. Given the urgency to increase agricultural production, continuation of the current program is too slow and expensive.

However, there is a viable option. Much greater use of the broadcast media, particularly radio, could be made. Since the majority of Ethiopians are illiterate, use of the broadcast media, in combination with other communication channels, could be very effective in technology dissemination. This would be strikingly cheap and effective in reaching farmers. Studies worldwide have shown that, in terms of cost per contact hour, extension workers are 2000 to 3500 times more expensive than radio.[17]

The government-controlled radio in Ethiopia, the most influential medium in reaching the rural population, does not usually provide educational content, nor inform rural people about programs directed at helping them. Rather the radio is used to disseminate government-sponsored political news and information. Private newspapers and other publications are not widely circulated in the country. Information flow is impeded by government control. According to the US Department of State, in 1996 only about one percent of the citizens of the country had regular access to any newspapers or magazines. Citizens outside the capital city of Addis Ababa have much more limited access to the print media because the most rural people are illiterate peasants. Distribution of newspapers and magazines from the independent press are effectively controlled by various and dubious means so the public does not understand what is going on in the country.

The operation of an effective extension service requires a regular supply of timely and appropriate messages directed to local extension workers and then to farmers by means of both audio-visual and printed materials so as to disseminate the results of research findings. The availability of such messages to the farming community has been proven to have a very positive impact on farmers' adoption of improved crop and livestock technology. Communication does not take over the function of the extension worker or the field development agent as is sometimes wrongly assumed. Rather it tries to help in the formulation of development strategies and activities, and in creating a communication environment in which it will be easier for the field development agent to work. Extension workers can encourage the formation of radio clubs where people can gather around a single receiver to listen to identified and recommended programs. Those who do not have radio receivers of their own thus have the opportunity to listen to the radio. These radio groups can be organized around the theme of *listen-discuss-act*. Radio broadcasts can be reinforced through village-based discussion groups that analyze the issues they hear on the radio, and prepare their responses/actions. Furthermore, members of these groups can ask for air time and, with the assistance of the extension worker, prepare a series of discussion, drama, or radio greetings clubs, for broadcast over the radio. Local media can serve as effective channels of communication between policy-makers and grassroots groups. As has been shown in Kenya and Tanzania, information on development can be channeled through district newspapers and community radio stations from the grassroots to policy-makers, and back to the grassroots. In the 1970s, in Homa Bay Kenya, the local radio station became the center of the community's self-help project communications network, offering development information and entertainment programming in the common vernacular language.

10.6 DSC Capacity-Building in Ethiopia

The government should make a discrete policy decision to build capacity in *Development Support Communication* throughout the government, and allocate adequate resources to accomplish that policy objective. With regard to capacity-building in Ethiopia, it is clear that much greater emphasis must be placed on the training of individuals to strengthen organizations to reinvigorate Ethiopian society.

A *Development Training and Communication Planning Center* should be established as an autonomous agency of the government. Its establishment as a *non-government* organization is preferable. It would be expected to play a vital role in moving forward the agricultural and rural sector by providing professional and technical advisory services to the government and its agencies. It would produce teaching/learning materials using Ethiopian prototypes or models to plan, organize and install *DSC* units in government offices and conduct in-service training of staff. There is clearly an urgent need to train agricultural and all other rural development workers at all levels on how to plan and more effectively use *Development Support Communication* in their programs.

All national training institutions should be strongly encouraged to build up their curricula in planning and management. These include the university's department of journalism and communication. University teaching programs in *Development Support Communication* are needed at both the undergraduate and graduate levels. Other national training institutions include the technical departments and schools teaching agriculture, extension education, community health, health education, sanitation, nutrition, environmental protection, and energy conservation.

Sources and Notes

[1] ECA/UN, *Communication for Participatory Development: A Training Manual*, (Economic Commission for Africa/United Nations, Addis Ababa, Ethiopia, 1994), p. 12.

[2] FAO, *Development Communication Paper: Perspectives on Communication for Rural Development*, (Food and Agricultural Organization/United Nations, Rome, Italy, 1987a), p. 3.

[3] FAO, *Development Support Communication: FAO Expert Consultation, June 8-12, 1987* (Food and Agricultural Organization, Rome, 1987b), p. (i).

[4] In this discussion, *change agent* is the generic term for any government or non-government village or other local development worker, including agricultural, health, or home extension agent.

[5] FAO, 1987b, op. cit., p. 2.

[6] John L. Wood and Romeo Gecolea, Proceedings of the *Regional Workshop on Development Support Communication for Rural Development*, (United Nations Development Program/Development Training and Communication Planning, Bangkok, Thailand, August 1982). p. 2. For purposes of this discussion, a *program* is comprised of one or more *projects*, and a *project* is comprised of one or more *activities*.

[7] M. K. D. Laswell, cited in *Participatory Development: A Training Manual*, No 1, (UN/ECA, Addis Ababa, Ethiopia, 1993), p. 13.

[8] John L. Wood and Romeo Gecolea, op. cit., p. 2.

[9] Also WHO established a special technical committee for health education in the early 1950s and continued to develop new guidelines and improvements in health education methods and strategies. Health education was declared the first and most continuous component of primary health care at the 1987 WHO-UNICEF Alma-Ata conference. Information, education, and communication is considered to be the single most important intervention for the control and prevention of HIV/AIDS in the WHO global program.

[10] FAO, 1987b, op. cit., p. 4.

[11] Ibid., p. 1.

[12] Multiple channels of communication may use elements from each of the media categories, including radio, television, newspaper, video film, slide film, audio cassettes, puppets and live theatre, and interpersonal channels such as group leaders and extension workers.

[13] For an objective appraisal of Ethiopia's major recent agricultural effort, see Julie Stepanek, Valerie Kelly, and Julie Howard, *From a Sasakawa Global 2000 Pilot Program to Sustained Increases in Agricultural Productivity: The Critical Role of Government Policy in Fostering the Ethiopian Transition*, (Selected Paper, American Agricultural Economics Association Annual Meeting, August 8-11, 1999, May 1999).

[14] Robert H. Bates, *Markets and States in Tropical Agriculture: The Political Basis of Agricultural Policies*, (University of California Press, Berkeley, California, 1984), p. 55.

[15] Julie Stepanek, Valerie Kelly, and Julie Howard, op. cit., p. 2.

[16] Theodore M. Vestal, *Ethiopia: A Post-Cold War African State*, (Praeger, London and Westport Connecticut, 1999), p. 74. Also see EPRDF, *Basic Facts: An Overview of Socio-Economic Development in Ethiopia,* (Ethiopian Peoples Revolutionary Democratic Front, Addis Ababa, First Quarter, 1999), p. 10.

[17] FAO, 1987a, op. cit., p. 5.

Chapter 11

Conclusion, a Strategy, and Interventions to Alleviate Rural Poverty

11.1 Conclusion

Prior to the 1960s, Ethiopia was usually self-sufficient in food production. However, by 1962, the country had become a net importer of cereals and flour. The development of its agriculture has been marred by a number of factors. Successive governments, with very different ideologies, have continued to implement wrong-headed policies that have militated against increases in agricultural productivity. General neglect of the agricultural sector and mishandling of tenancy and land reform issues are particularly noteworthy. For most of the past four decades, development of the agricultural sector has received less than two percent of successive governments' annual budget allocations. To most observers, this seems incomprehensible, given the dominance of agriculture in Ethiopia's economy. Even today, over three-quarters of all Ethiopians are employed in agriculture; it provides over one-half of the nation's GDP, and over two-thirds of its total foreign exchange earnings. Moreover, it provides most of the raw materials for its industry and food for its citizens.

Throughout Ethiopia, small farmers have lacked the means to improve their productivity. This is the result of land tenure issues, fragmented holdings, lack of improved crop production technology and credit for inputs, paucity of input and product markets, and the absence of adequate physical infrastructure, especially roads, schools and health centers. The insecurity of tenure and high rents killed the peasants' incentives to increase production. Beginning in the 1960s, commercial farms were established in some areas, mostly near the Rift Valley lakes and in the Awash Valley. Most of these farms were efficient and profitable; producing mainly export crops such as sugar cane, cotton, fruits, and vegetables. The policy of the Imperial Government was to promote commercial agriculture because of economies of scale. Investors in commercial agriculture were allowed to import duty-free tractors and harvesting combines, fuel, spare parts and chemicals. Ethiopia's meager foreign exchange resources were spent in this way, while the peasant sector was totally neglected. Still, commercial farming has remained in its infancy. Even today subsistence crop and livestock provide some 90 percent of total agricultural output.

Commencing in 1967, the Imperial Government in collaboration with the Swedish International Development Agency introduced the "package approach" in the Chilalo Agricultural Development Unit (CADU). It was envisaged that if the improved agricultural technologies tried on the project's research facility and smallholder farms were successful, they would be diffused to other areas by means of model farmers working under extension agents. The CADU project succeeded in increasing the income of beneficiaries through new technologies that increased crop production, but numerous other problems arose. The increased returns from the credit program, as well as from extension and marketing services, drove land rents up by 33 to 50 percent. In some cases, tenants were evicted in large numbers to make way for mechanized farms. So the benefits went largely to the landlords rather than to the disadvantaged tenants and other small farmers. This was particularly true in densely populated highland areas where, although otherwise intended, there was virtually no smallholder participation in the planning and implementation of the project. The Ministry of Agriculture did most planning from the "top down" in collaboration with the Swedish aid agency. Tenants were required to present a written leasehold agreement signed by the landlord that was accepted by CADU whose marketing division sold fertilizer to peasant farmers in cash. It goes without saying that cash buyers were only the relatively wealthy farmers. The poorer small farmers who comprised the majority of rural people were excluded.

In 1971, the Imperial Government launched the Minimum Package Program (MPP) as a new strategy for the large-scale diffusion of some of the success experiences of the CADU and other "package projects." The intent was to distribute implements, other crop production inputs, oxen, and credit to various groups of peasant farmers. Although the MPP improved the agricultural productivity of small-scale farmers, particularly in the existing project areas, there were many problems associated with discrimination of small farmers elsewhere. The restrictive credit system favored large landowners and encouraged eviction of tenants. Those who met the credit requirements were able to see immediate benefits of the MPP. Others interested in participating in the MPP were unable to make the down payment, and tenants were frustrated when their landlords refused to sign credit contracts for them.

The land reform issue was not addressed until after the 1974 military revolution. By the early 1970s, Emperor Haile Selassie was growing senile and gradually losing control. Furthermore, wealthy feudal landlords surrounded him. It is clear that no serious land reform could have been undertaken during his reign, although there was mounting pressure for land reform from multilateral and bilateral donor agencies and countries. The Emperor's inability to implement meaningful land reform and general neglect of the peasant sector, coupled with the famine conditions in 1973, contributed to Ethiopia's general social and economic deterioration and the overthrow of his regime. Unmindful of the heavy tolls which the famine claimed, and unwilling to acknowledge the magnitude and intensity of suffering, Haile Selassie's government treated this human tragedy with the utmost secrecy and gross negligence.

In March 1975, the Ethiopian ruling military council proclaimed sweeping land reform measures. These included allowing peasants to organize themselves into peasant associations to implement the land reform measures, including land redistribution, litigation, administration of public property and promotion of cooperative schemes and development projects. The reform program abolished the landlord-tenant relationship and private ownership of land. No compensation was offered to former landowners. A farm family was allowed access to a maximum of ten hectares of land. The land was not to be sold, leased, mortgaged or disposed of in any form, but its use right was inheritable. Commercial farms and estates became state farms.

Making all rural lands "the collective property of the Ethiopian people" was seen as a solution to the farmland ownership-concentration problem. However, the reform program overlooked the historical significance of private ownership of land in Ethiopia and its impact on incentives to produce. Nonetheless, the land reform freed the peasantry from an obligation to pay rents and tributes, and provided guaranteed access to land. The measures also destroyed the landlord class, and peasant associations became the basic unit of political power. The reform measures initially improved the living conditions of smallholder families. This was because the added production of food gained as a result of land reform was consumed on the farm. However, the quantity of food that was surplus to the farm household's consumption needs and so marketed sharply declined.

Therefore, the urgent problem faced by the military government was how to increase the volume of marketed output for urban consumers and the army as rapidly as possible. The most practical approach was to rapidly expand the state farm sector since most of the output of this sector was marketable. Unfortunately, yields on state farms were about the same as yields in the peasant sector although their use of scarce production inputs was much higher. The state farms thus consumed an enormous portion of the public resources available for agriculture and accumulated large debts. Donor agencies and countries criticized the government's emphasis on large-scale state farms and the neglect of the peasant sector while the donors necessarily channeled their agricultural aid to the smallholder sector. The donors rightly maintained that experience elsewhere in Africa, in Eastern Europe and the Soviet Union had shown that state farms were inefficient and a drain on scarce resources.

The military government's stated objective was to transform the entire peasant sector into a cooperative and then collective farm sector. Peasant farms were the dominant type of production unit in Ethiopian agriculture, covering about 95 percent of the nation's cultivated land. The producer cooperatives performed no better than peasant farms in terms of production, nor did they improve the living standards of their members to any significant extent. Several factors explain the Marxist-Leninist's preference for collective farming models, whether state farms or cooperatives with extensive state direction. Cooperative or collective farms are more amenable to state control. State bureaucracies can more readily enforce decisions about what crops are grown and what price they sell for. Collectivization has also been seen as a tool for eradicating *bourgeois* tendencies among the peasantry. Finally, state planners have insisted that larger, centralized collective farms are more efficient than smallholder agriculture. Thus the military government ordered the creation of producer cooperatives, although efforts to persuade the peasantry to form producer cooperatives did not meet with a great deal of success. Even with inducements and various types of incentives provided by the government, farmers responded less than enthusiastically. They saw the move to form cooperatives as a prelude to the destruction of their "family farms."

The resistance of peasant farmers to producer cooperatives caused the government to implement resettlement and villagization programs. Here too, the military government claimed that resettlement would resolve the country's recurring drought problems and would ease population pressure from northern areas where the land had been badly overused. The rationale for resettlement programs was valid, but the government's intention to settle 1.5 million people by the year 1984 was certainly unrealistic and overly ambitious. Ethiopia simply did not have the resources or the capacity to implement it. Moreover, there were human rights violations, forced separation of families and lack of medical attention in resettlement centers that resulted in thousands of deaths from various ailments and lack of basic sanitary conditions.

Another ambitious military government program was that of "villagization." The objectives of moving scattered farm households into villages were rational land use, provision of clean water and health and educational services, and strengthened physical security. Few impact and evaluative studies of villagization are available. However, it is known that villagization was also intended to enhance the control of the state over the rural population, and eventually convert those villages into agricultural collectives or agricultural communes.

Leadership from within Ethiopia created most of Ethiopia's economic problems of the last four decades. Its poor record in terms of economic development is the result of lack of political commitment for change; urban-focused economic policies; government control, corruption, and mismanagement of resources; attempted micromanagement of economic activities; and regulation of the lives of its people. Rural-focused economic policy reform continues to be a matter of urgency in Ethiopia in its long journey toward sustainable economic maturity. Such economic reform, particularly in agriculture, is essential to produce the growth and rural transformation that Ethiopia must have to provide for the basic needs of its citizens. Rural-focused economic policy reform would surely have tangible and dramatic impact on food production and poverty alleviation.

11.2 A Strategy for Poverty Alleviation

Ethiopia, with the majority of its population still comprised of smallholder farm families, is still in an early stage of structural transformation. Structural transformation is the process whereby a predominately agrarian economy is transformed into a diversified and productive economy dominated by value-added processing, manufacturing, and services. Nation states in this early stage can be characterized by low incomes, low levels of productivity, limited growth of off-farm employment, and high fertility and population growth rates.[1] Ethiopia may be unique in the sense that it has suffered more than most nations in recent decades from political instability and civil strife, weak governance, corruption and mismanagement, and a paucity of human and institutional capital – all of which have contributed to its failure to achieve broad-based economic growth.

Furthermore, until this decade, Ethiopia was affected by the distorting effects of the Cold War on the priorities of donors, as well as the ready availability of food aid. With a more stable security and political situation since the current government assumed power in 1991, Ethiopia has had the opportunity to address the constraints to advancing its economy and its society. However, the current government's record to date has been mixed.

Given the above, it is most appropriate that highest priority be given to implementing a major *small farmer-led agricultural and rural development strategy* to address the low levels of productivity of both food and cash crops in the dominant small farmer sector. The focus must be on what Carl Eicher has described as "the five prime movers of agricultural development," namely:

- A *favorable economic environment* that flows from a political system which promotes, defends, and protects the economic interests of farmers and rural people.
- *Human capability* and managerial skills that are created through formal education, training and on-the-job-experience.
- *New technology* that is generated, tested and diffused to farmers.
- *Rural capital formation* such as physical capital (roads, irrigation, dams) and biological capital (improved livestock herds).
- *Rural institutions* such as credit, seed multiplication and marketing.[2]

Only by raising the productivity of the small farmer can food security and sustained broad-based economic growth be attained. The agricultural development experience in Africa, and elsewhere, clearly indicates that labor-extensive increases in farm labor productivity must be supported by an effective small farmer-oriented system to develop and distribute new technologies. Also as small farmer output increases, much more attention must be given to the provision of production credit for improved inputs, reducing post-harvest losses, marketing, processing, and rural infrastructure that support agriculture.[3]

In this study, the development crises of last four decades under three very different political and economic systems – the feudalistic agrarian, the command economy, and the current laissez-faire – were examined and compared. This study has examined the progressive social and economic decay from the 1960s to 1990s. From that experience, we can learn numerous lessons, all indicating the need to raise the productivity of small farmers. It is clear that Ethiopia must formulate a policy framework directed at supporting implementation of a major *small farmer-led agricultural and rural development strategy*.

A *small farmer-led agricultural and rural development strategy* is consistent with the current government's statements. These statements focus on increasing production and diversifying food crops to provide food security, as well as the increasing production and diversifying cash crops for export from which foreign exchange earnings are generated. Regretfully, as indicated in Chapter 6 and elsewhere in this study, the current government's actions with regard to agricultural and rural development do not match its rhetoric. Furthermore, the political environment created by the current government encouraging ethnic divisiveness is a major constraint to implementing a broad-based economic development strategy.

11.3 Interventions Required to Alleviate Rural Poverty

Implementing a *small farmer-led agricultural and rural development strategy* directed at broad-based economic development in Ethiopia requires a major effort on the part of both the private and public sectors. The following are the most important specific interventions needed to implement such a strategy.

Investment in Smallholder Agriculture

Given that agriculture remains the principal economic activity of the majority of the rural population in Ethiopia, raising agricultural output is the most efficient way of achieving food security while raising rural income and living standards. The importance of increasing the productivity of smallholder agriculture was stressed in the African

Heads of States and Governments' 1980 "Lagos Plan of Action," and the OAU's 1986 "Priorities for Economic Recovery." Also the World Bank's 1981 "Agenda for Action" and 1989 "From Crisis to Sustainable Development," as well as the FAO African Regional Conference's 1984 "Harare Declaration on the Food Crisis in Africa," strongly recommended that priority be accorded smallholder agriculture in achieving food security and food self-sufficiency in Africa.[4]

For agriculture to move forward, Ethiopia needs to increase public sector investment in agriculture to some 20-25 percent of its budget as was pledged by African leaders in 1989. With radical increases in agricultural investment, with incentives for farmers to produce more, and the development and dissemination of improved production technology, Ethiopia could easily feed itself again. Quite clearly it has the physical and human resources to produce significantly more food. Moreover, modernization of agriculture would have great impact on national life. A major policy reorientation toward increasing domestic food production is needed. Raising the output and incomes of the peasant sector during this new millennium via a *small farmer-led agricultural and rural development strategy* must be of the highest priority.

During the crucial period of the next decade, Ethiopian farmers must increase their output at a sustained rate of four percent per annum to feed the new mouths and maintain the current living standards. Only if Ethiopia's farmers are encouraged to prosper through the provision of practical assistance as discussed below, can the foundation for national development be established. A substantial advancement in Ethiopian smallholder agriculture will depend upon a favorable policy environment; development and widespread diffusion of improved technologies; and access to institutional credit, inputs, and marketing services. In many areas, irrigation development, reforestation, and soil and water conservation efforts will also be required. This can be achieved by raising the proportion of government recurrent and capital expenditure going to support agricultural and rural development activities. Rural infrastructure, roads, schools, health centers, and rural electrification will also require additional attention over time.

The alternative, as experienced elsewhere in the world and witnessed by Ethiopians under the previous dictatorial regime, could again lead Ethiopia to massive economic chaos, and expose Ethiopians to more starvation, poverty, and despair. It is clear that there can be little hope for broad-based economic development unless the primary emphasis is on smallholder agricultural development.

Rural Savings and Access to Credit

For modernization of agriculture, savings and rural credit are key elements. To increase production, farmers must have funds to purchase physical inputs – fertilizer, improved seeds, pesticides, and labor. The informal sector, comprised of merchants, middlemen, and the private moneylenders, is today the main source of funds for small farmers and rural entrepreneurs. They charge excessively high interest rates. On the other hand, formal lending institutions have rigid requirements and are reluctant to give loans to small farmers and women entrepreneurs because they lack the necessary collateral and are considered "high risk". In fact, loans to small-scale borrowers are not necessarily more risky. There is no inverse correlation between amount of the loan and degree of risk, and the proportion of bad and doubtful debts is no higher among small farmers and small business persons.

However, the majority of small farmers and small business persons are reluctant to borrow from financial institutions because of the cumbersome and time-consuming procedures applied by lending institutions. Creating a more flexible set of rules and regulations under which credit can be granted is a necessary step. Banking practices for agricultural credit and savings should be made more appropriate and simplified to improve application and loan approval procedures, collateral security requirements, and personnel policies – all with a focus on small-scale peasant farmers and entrepreneurs. More banking personnel should be trained and located in rural branches, and more qualified agricultural loan personnel should be recruited to identify viable farming projects.

Savings mobilization schemes can strengthen local financial institutions and reduce their dependence on government. Rural savings mobilization activities should be encouraged to promote the use of banks as a habit through the provision of deposit facilities. Such facilities rarely exist in rural settings in Ethiopia. In dealing with savings and credit activities, it is always important that saving comes first and credit comes second. This will ensure effective rural resources mobilization and provide a vehicle for the creation of credit for peasant farmers and small-scale entrepreneurs.

The time has come for a new economic policy on rural financing. To provide for its rural credit needs, the federal government must establish an *Agricultural Credit Guarantee Program Fund* as an incentive for banks to finance agriculture. Ethiopia needs to improve its efforts at savings mobilization and thereby increase its access to development finance. The provision of credit, using the group-guarantee system, rather than land for collateral, has proven effective together with other measures designed to generate off-farm employment. These include support for training, marketing and small agriculturally-based processing enterprises. The government in cooperation with local financial institutions needs to develop a more rational savings/lending policy where poor farmers and peasants who produce the bulk of the food in the country would have relatively greater access to formal financial markets. The ability to borrow money to engage in legitimate business activity must therefore be facilitated by banks and other credit-granting agencies. This means that access to credit must be improved. The best way of improving access is through group savings and credit as demonstrated in other African and Asian nations.

Participatory Development Planning and Implementation

Policies and programs designed in government ministries and agencies with little or no participation of the rural poor have resulted in the failure of these policies and programs that were intended to alleviate poverty and construct a path to sustainable development. Development projects cannot be successful if conceived in isolation from rural people, based only on physical or economic data. Participation of the targeted beneficiaries from the initial stages of the planning of a project is crucial for the project to meet its stated objectives. Villagers must be consulted and assisted in developing improved means of food production while preserving and harnessing their farming potential. If planners, administrators and managers acknowledge this basic principle before attempting to implement projects, fewer resources and effort would be wasted. It must be clear that rural people have their own ideas, information, knowledge, technical capabilities, and leadership qualities. They must be given opportunities and considered as participants rather than only beneficiaries in joint endeavors to improve their productivity and welfare. Without the active involvement of the local people and their organizations in the development process, sustained improvement of human levels of living cannot be achieved.

The 1990 African Charter for Popular Participation in Development affirmed this by calling for an era in which the participation and empowerment of the ordinary men and women are the order of the day. The Charter attested to the fact that people's participation must be at the heart of Africa's development mission and vision, and it confirmed that authentic development springs from the collective imagination, experience, and decisions of people. For the participatory process to be effective, both political and economic power must be held by people within their communities. Experience shows that policy-makers cannot command effective participation. It must instead be induced through the advocacy of projects that offer sufficient incentives to attract the personal resources of time, energy, and freedom of action away from other urgent and competing tasks of the common people.

Development Support Communication

Development Support Communication (DSC) is a relatively new activity and has been evolving rapidly as an academic discipline that has useful applications for development efforts. It helps rural people acquire knowledge and skills, and promotes information exchange at and between all levels in a development intervention. Through DSC, it is possible to organize and manage systems to promote horizontal communication (among planners, technicians, groups of people). And it is possible to promote vertical communication (from planners to the grass-roots level and feedback from the grass-roots level to planners).

For DSC to be successful it must take into account the perspectives of the rural people, and it must be incorporated in the planning and programming stages of projects. A DSC activity requires a critical mass of resources, communication staff, and equipment below which little or no impact can be expected. Four or five years should be considered the usual time frame for a DSC activity.

Policy makers should recognize the role of communication in increasing the efficiency, cost effectiveness and continuity of development activities. The strategic use of communication for development requires a policy decision in favor of broad-based communication support for rural development, using all media infrastructure available to it in an orchestrated fashion. This gives better results than concentration on one medium, such as only radio broadcasting or newspapers.

The strategic use of communication for development requires substantial government support. Such support includes the training in communication skills of research scientists, communication specialists, planners, administrators and managers, and even policy-makers. Courses in development communication are not offered anywhere in Ethiopia, nor is there a DSC training center. Therefore, university teaching programs in DSC are needed at the bachelor, masters, and doctoral levels. National training institutions such as departments of journalism and communication, and technical departments of schools teaching agriculture, health education, extension education, environmental studies, community health, nutrition, and sanitation should be approached to build up their curricula in the area of development communication planning and management. The production of information, education, and communication materials for training in communication skills must also be accorded high priority in designing DSC projects. Government should also provide assistance in systematic planning and implementation of communication as an integral component of development programs and projects, including the training of government communication officers.

Crop Production Technologies

Recurrent and prolonged droughts have ravaged Ethiopia for many generations, and adoption of location-specific packages of improved technology, including fertilizer and high yielding seed varieties that are resistant to drought, have the potential for dramatic increases in agricultural production. This is already apparent in some locations. Yet relatively few resources are being directed at building the agricultural research capacity to generate and test the stream of new technology needed to sustain such increases in production. Particularly, much more research is needed on traditional crops. *Enset* for instance, which looks like a large, thick, single-stemmed banana plant, helped people living in southern Ethiopia escape the worst effects of the deadly famines in the 1970s and 1980s. Encouraging farmers in drought prone areas to grow the crops of *enset* would provide insurance against circumstances that often lead to famine. *Enset* is not famine-proof, but it prevents people from experiencing the usual suffering associated with famine conditions. Other traditional crops requiring more research are sorghum, millet, cassava, bananas, and yams. Ethiopians should be encouraged to develop a taste for cassava, yams and green vegetables rather than depending almost solely on *teff.* These vegetable crops have been cultivated intensively in Ethiopia's neighboring countries, and have proven their resistance to pests and drought conditions.

Livestock Production

Ethiopia is endowed with the largest number of livestock in Africa, and ranks tenth in size in the world. The livestock sub-sector consists mainly cattle, sheep, goats, horses, mules, donkeys, camels, and poultry. Some 20 percent of the GDP is provided by the livestock sub-sector. The export of livestock and livestock products make an important contribution to foreign exchange earnings of the country. Next to coffee, the export of live animals, processed leather and shoes, meat, dairy products, eggs, and hides and skins is the largest contributor to Ethiopian foreign exchange earnings. Even so, the contribution of this sub-sector to the national economy has not nearly reached its potential. This is due mainly to under-nutrition and malnutrition, the prevalence of animal diseases and parasites, as well as the lack of veterinary services, adequate animal feed, water, transport, and livestock husbandry and management skills.

Animals must have access to adequate food, water and shelter and be treated humanely. They must also have access to veterinary services and improved husbandry. Livestock owners must be given training and on-site technical advice to improve their knowledge of animal care, breeding, and management. To realize the potential of the livestock resource, alleviate rural poverty, and sustain the environment, formulation and implementation of a discrete strategy for development of the livestock sub-sector should be given high priority.

Rural Women in Development

It should be recognized that gender is an important factor in the success of any development effort and women participants should always be included, even in livestock production. Women usually care for animals kept near the house, but often have little access to technical training, resources, and credit. When women receive animals and training, family nutrition improves, and women gain new respect in their communities. Through women, improved nourishment, increased production, and the dissemination of skills and knowledge for self-reliance can strengthen rural communities.

Women in Ethiopia, as in all of sub-Saharan Africa, play a pivotal role in the economic development of the country. However, the important role of women in the agricultural labor force, public works, family health, and energy and deforestation issues has not been widely recognized. Even though women hold some senior government positions, in practice they do not enjoy equal status with men. The law holds men and women to be equal, but tradition and cultural factors place the man as head of the household. Discrimination is most acute among the 85 percent of the population living in the rural areas, where women work over 13 hours a day fulfilling household and farming responsibilities. In urban areas, women have fewer employment opportunities than men do, and the jobs available do not provide equal working conditions or pay. Ethiopian women contribute much to the national economy, producing an estimated 60 to 80 percent of crops. They are also the primary processors and marketers of food supplies consumed in the country. The roles of women in the household and economy require more attention. Any development strategy must encourage the poverty-alleviating efforts of women. There can be no successful development efforts, no effective poverty-alleviation initiatives, unless the needs of women are directly addressed.

Saving the Environment

Ethiopia suffers from a variety of environmental problems. The most urgent issues requiring attention are deforestation, massive extinction of wildlife and plant species, depletion of ancient water-producing aquifers and erosion of agricultural soils. Among these, the most serious has contributed much to the recurring droughts and desertification. It is the continuing soil degradation due to the excessive exploitation of land by over-grazing, over-cultivation and deforestation. At present, the forest reserves in Ethiopia are estimated to be less than three percent. About 100,000 hectares of forests are reportedly lost annually. As a consequence, firewood and coal, which supply 90 percent of domestic energy, are dwindling. The loss of topsoil implies a general deterioration of agriculture because this loss cannot be compensated for by increased applications of fertilizer. Therefore, natural resources such as forests, land, soil, water, and minerals must be protected and utilized in sustainable manner. There must be clear guidelines regarding tree ownership, incentives for individual ventures in tree planting, community participation, and the benefits to be derived from afforestation activities. For reasons that are difficult to explain, the generally agreed need for tree planting on a massive scale remains in the talking stage between local administrations and donor agencies. It is essential that afforestation and reforestation programs be strongly supported by leaders in successive Ethiopian governments. They should be "pet" programs of Ethiopia's leaders. A nationwide campaign, *zemecha,* is sorely needed. The current government cannot afford to delay action on afforestation and reforestation any longer. Its goal should be to regain at least the 100,000 hectares lost annually through soil erosion as described above. The government should heavily involve peasant associations, as well as women and youth organizations. Regions requiring special attention are Tigray, Gondar, Wollo, Shoa, Hararge and Sidamo. To date no programs to rehabilitate the northern areas of famine have received serious consideration or investment.

A special day should be set aside once a year for nationwide tree planting led by the head of state to raise the level of consciousness and to educate the Ethiopian public with regard to how vital tree planting is for Ethiopian environmental protection. The Ethiopian government should convene its first "national environmental conference" to inform the Ethiopian public and donor community about the deepening crisis of the environment in Ethiopia, and formulate policy guidelines for environmental protection. The Government should also establish an environmental agency with national, regional and local offices, and a research institution with capacity at selected locations. The guidelines should encourage private initiatives in planting trees and allow private ownership of trees via peasant associations, as well as women and youth organizations. The mass media should be used to widely publicize the conference and its results. In the past, the authority to undertake afforestation and reforestation efforts was delegated more to government agencies, and less to peasant farm families, or other local people and their institutions. The result was that a great deal of human and capital resources committed to the afforestation and reforestation efforts had only marginal impact. The new policy guidelines should give more power and permit active participation of local people through their organizations, particularly the peasant associations.

In past decades, "food for work" projects have raised millions of tree seedlings, terraced and planted seedlings on many thousands of hectares of land. To what extent these programs have continued to be implemented is unclear, but these programs certainly need to be further developed and greatly expanded by the present regime. The government should give high priority to working with peasant associations to launch tree-planting campaigns, as well as assure tree survival in the drought-prone provinces of the north and northwest, namely Tigray, Gondar, Gojjam, Wollo, Shoa. The peasant associations that were involved in land redistribution, as well as development programs aimed at increasing agricultural production during the time of the military government, could be used to mobilize and motivate local farmers, women groups, and youth. They could be mobilized to participate in tree planting, water, and land conservation, and in keeping the environment a safer place to live. Irrigation projects have obvious appeal and can compensate for erratic rainfall. However, large-scale drainage and irrigation efforts require very high capital expenditures. Although the focus must be on small-farmer development, large schemes for dry land farming, and large and small-scale irrigation development all have their place in the agricultural future of Ethiopia. A system of rainwater collection and reservoirs would be particularly useful for irrigation in the dry season on hilly slopes.

Land tenure is one of the major contributing factors to the failure of the reforestation efforts. The current land tenure policy does not give the necessary incentives to farmers. It should be changed if people are to invest in rural areas to promote economic growth. The lack of clearly defined property rights, "the common property problem" or "the tragedy of the commons," has contributed to land degradation and deforestation over the last quarter of a century. There is also no coherent national forestry policy in Ethiopia, a point that has significantly contributed to excessive deforestation and soil erosion. To correct this deficiency, there should be a national forestry policy that would give adequate incentives for individuals, groups, and communities to invest in the production of trees and tree products. Such a development strategy would require the formulation of new policies and legislation that would permit active participation of the peasantry through the peasant associations in soil and water conservation projects.

The state ownership of land has had a damaging impact on the environment by contributing to accelerating deforestation. Some of the most severe environmental degradation in the world today is found in the ex-communist states, and it is directly related to the lack of property and land ownership rights. Without security of tenure, farmers do not have incentives to conserve the environment through activities such as planting trees, or to otherwise make significant permanent improvements on their land.

Land Tenure

Land tenure is still a major issue in Ethiopia. The "land to the tiller" cry of students a generation ago is a policy that has yet to be implemented. The 1975 land reform proclamation of the military government made all rural lands the "collective property" of all Ethiopians. It replaced the power of the landlord and the moneylender in the countryside with the power of the state. It is only when people gain control over productive assets that they will be able to produce to reduce the level of poverty and eradicate widespread hunger and starvation. The current rural and urban land policy of the Ethiopian government is not conducive to investment in agriculture or in urban centers. It must be replaced by a policy that clearly defines property rights. Land reform is essential to empower local farmers and reduce insecurity of land tenure. If agriculture is to be the engine of economic growth, the distribution of land to all cultivators as private property is a necessary condition for economic development. The denial of access to land ownership for Ethiopian citizens, if left for too long, could have serious consequences for agricultural production and rural welfare. Research shows that in those nations where individual rights are preserved, economic growth rates are about twice those of nations where such rights are strained. The collapse of the Soviet and Eastern

European communist states and China's remarkable economic transformation have inspired market-oriented reforms in other state-dominated economies. For example, Vietnam has transferred state farmland to the peasantry and freed prices from state control.

The position usually presented by EPRDF government, and the military government before it, is that allowing private ownership of land might result in a possible return of the former landowners who might then expropriate land from peasant cultivators. There is no evidence to support this position. It is absolutely ridiculous for the government to continue to disseminate such false propaganda. The simple truth is that the purpose of this policy is to allow the government to control the national wealth and to make the average Ethiopian citizen more dependent on the government. The issue of land ownership has been lingering for more than four decades and the lack of property rights is one of the major obstacles to agricultural growth. The issue of ownership should not be decided by urban elites, but should be decided with the full involvement of the peasant beneficiaries. If a referendum were held today, the Ethiopian peasantry would prefer private ownership by individuals over other forms of ownership to further agricultural modernization.

Land Resettlement

Land resettlement has been a means of generating employment and income during successive regimes in Ethiopia. It has been successfully implemented in Africa, Latin America, and the Middle East, including Israel. The resettlement program introduced by the *Derg* during the 1984 drought as an antidote for famine caused worldwide criticism and condemnation as the program was politically and ideologically motivated. New settlements were incorporated into the structure of the All-Ethiopian Peasant Associations, and eventually organized into producers' cooperatives. The military government's promise to provide the settlers with ten hectares of land, housing, farm equipment, oxen, food, and even clothing until a crop was harvested never materialized. Peasants were rounded up and moved into settlement areas against their will. It is estimated that 50 to 100 thousand of those resettled died as a result of the difficult conditions at the settlement sites.

This does not necessarily mean that Ethiopia should not consider a voluntary resettlement program in the future. Ethiopia's dependence on food aid and commercial grain imports has increased considerably over the last few years. Instead of claiming that hunger in Ethiopia has been eliminated, the current government should attempt to attack poverty on every front, including through land resettlement programs.

Unemployment is a very serious problem in Ethiopia, and the opportunities to find non-agricultural jobs are few. Since there is productive land not being cultivated, resettlement has potential to provide employment, reduce poverty, as well as address the food security problem. The government's announcement that the country had already attained full food self-sufficiency (after only one year of good harvests) may harden the attitudes of the donors at this time when there are new pleas for external food assistance. It is tragic that in the year 2000, some eleven million Ethiopians in the south and southeast were at risk of starvation.

Human Capital Development

In Ethiopia one of the worst bottlenecks to economic development has proven to be the shortage of trained personnel. Training institutions for professional and para-professionals must be established in large numbers, augmented, and strengthened. The effect on poverty of not having these training institutions is sometimes indirect – but always critical. Alleviating poverty demands improvements in human infrastructure – through training for both the general population and for professional and para-professional elites. Unfortunately, the institutions to prepare them are not yet in place. Budgetary and other resources for education in Ethiopia are among the lowest in Africa. Hence it is crucial to give increased attention to education directed at increasing the human capital to strengthen and build the capacity of development institutions.

Off-Farm and Non-Agricultural Rural Activities

The objective of providing a decent standard of living for the country's rural population cannot be accomplished through reliance on the agricultural sector alone. Over time, as small farmer productivity increases, there will be diversification from agriculture to off-farm agricultural and non-agricultural activities in the rural areas. Those activities not only create additional employment opportunities and alternative occupations for the rural poor, but also provide higher income to farmers selling their output to agricultural industries and to those engaged in such activities. Supporting small-enterprise development with financial assistance and entrepreneurial training will contribute to creating job opportunities and generating income.

Financial and credit programs are important instruments for the development of small enterprises, but access to funds and services is often very limited. Financial institutions and banks can play important roles in these programs. In view of the growing demands for financing small enterprise, more lending institutions should be established in the rural areas of Ethiopia. Non-governmental organizations (NGO's) can be vital links between the formal financing system and micro-entrepreneurs. For instance in Kenya, the Kenya Women Finance Trust, a local NGO, with a mission to finance and train women entrepreneurs, has cooperated with financial institutions in developing tailor-made programs to induce business-like approaches and professional attitudes to improve the quality of their programs.

Direct government intervention in the private sector must by all means be discouraged. However, there are numerous ways in which the government can be supportive indirectly. One way is to see that more people have access to adequate financing and small-business support services. This can be achieved by providing incentives to financial institutions to invest significant resources in small-business activities aimed at generating employment and income for the poor. In financing micro-projects, it is important to emphasize projects that directly benefit the poor. Such projects include oil mills, flourmills, cottage industries, sewing, poultry, piggeries, transport, brick making, and rug making.

Relief and Reconstruction Efforts for the Poor

Providing emergency relief after a country has been devastated by famine or a similar calamity is one thing. Reconstructing and rebuilding the economy from A to Z is another. What has been lacking in Ethiopia during the last four decades has been the latter. In order to eradicate absolute poverty, the government needs to pursue direct anti-poverty efforts. There should be a program for direct alleviation of poverty through employment-generating projects. Such projects include small-scale irrigation works, land reclamation, soil conservation, afforestation, rural roads, and small buildings. Another type of program for direct alleviation of poverty could be community-initiated projects. These are projects identified and implemented by the communities themselves, e.g., building schools and health centers, water-sanitation facilities, and agricultural infrastructure.

In the 1970s and 1980s, integrated rural development projects were implemented to alleviate rural poverty in many countries around the world. The approach sought to assist targeted groups below the poverty line through various kinds of asset transfer, especially land, with mixed success. Poor rural beneficiaries could engage in income-producing enterprises such as livestock or crop production and be lifted above the poverty level on a sustained basis. It is very crucial that any such activities in Ethiopia include specific programs for rural employment, and for the development of dry farming areas that benefit small farmers, marginal farmers and landless agricultural laborers.

Population and Family Planning

The factors that cause food insecurity are several. Poverty remains a primary cause. A second major cause is the rapid rate of population growth. Ethiopia's total population was estimated at 60 million in 1997, and is expected to double to 120 million by the year 2021. At a three-percent annual growth rate, Ethiopia will have to feed some 2 million new mouths every year. Mortality on the other hand has been dropping continuously due to improved medical facilities and nutritional intake, and modest improvements in the standard of living. Historically, the effect of a growing population was countered by an increase in the rate of food production. Unfortunately, for four decades food production has not kept up with increases in population. Thus it is crucial to give greater priority to promoting family planning efforts that will reduce fertility rates of women in their childbearing years. The use of modern contraceptives to allow child spacing has great potential in accelerating Ethiopia's demographic transition. Family planning coverage has reached a mere two percent of women in their childbearing years, and only 16 percent of pregnant women register for prenatal care. This situation could be reversed if women health workers were trained and women associations organized at the village level to effectively disseminate family planning information.

Growth with Equity and Basic Human Needs

It has now become commonplace to read that the economies of such countries as Kenya, Ghana, Botswana, and South Africa have been doing well, as evidenced by annual GNP growth rates of five to eight percent in recent years. Far less attention has been focused on how that growth was distributed among its citizens with the objective of reducing urban and rural poverty. That important dimension indicates that the most appropriate development strategy must assure "growth with equity". Therefore, a *basic human needs* strategy is most appropriate. Experience in other developing countries has demonstrated clearly that countries with more evenly distributed income from broad-based economic growth have grown faster than those with more highly skewed incomes. *Basic human needs* involves safe drinking water, adequate food, shelter, and clothing, proper sanitation and health facilities, reasonable housing, education, and employment opportunities. Until recently, military dictatorships dominated most African states with limited opportunities for citizens to voice their concerns. Today the number of countries that have introduced democracy in their countries is increasing – Nigeria being one of the latest.

Ethnic Regionalism

Following the seizure of power by the TPLF in May 1991, Ethiopia was divided into 14 ethnically homogenous territories (*killils*) on the basis of language. The TPLF created ethnic-based puppet political parties under the umbrella organization of the EPRDF, the ruling party in Ethiopia. Consistent with its ethnic policy, the TPLF/EPRDF has to date excluded the major non-ethnic ideology-based political groups. This is a policy of "divide and rule." However, to attempt to draw clear boundaries around ethnic groups is to attempt the impossible. The consequence must necessarily be to create havoc and suffering, ethnic hatred, and to intensify ethnic conflict. One international authority who participated in the Constitutional Commission held in Addis Ababa in 1992 accurately reported:

> Drawing regional boundaries along ethnic lines...supplements what is an avoidable with what is undesirable...the combination of ethnic territorial units and ethnic parties cumulative cleavages (sic) and can have a disastrous effect on national unity and political stability.[5]

Ethiopia needs peace and stability to move forward. Regretfully, it has yet to develop a democratic political culture that includes the willingness to accept electoral defeat, a tolerance of opposition groups and viewpoints, and the ability of contending factions to cooperate. To build a new Ethiopia, there must first be reconciliation, rule of law, multi-party democracy and pluralism, private property rights, and respect for human rights. The greatest challenge for the current rulers in Ethiopia is to promote ethnic and national reconciliation, and nurture and exploit the full benefits of diversity. The current policy of the EPRDF creates division rather than unity in diversity.

11.4 A Note on the Ethiopian-Eritrean War[6]

It is indeed sad that two of the poorest countries in the world, namely Ethiopia and Eritrea, have been engaged in an armed conflict since mid-1998. Both countries rely heavily on international humanitarian aid. They have severe budgetary and foreign exchange constraints. Yet they have bought huge quantities of arms from Russia and Ukraine. Meanwhile their citizens' basic human needs are unmet, and their economic development efforts are severely under-funded. Yet it is estimated that Ethiopia has quadrupled its defense spending since the war began to US $467 million in 1999. After a similar increase, Eritrea spent US $236 million in 1999.

The war began in May 1998, as a clash over an obscure area of borderland. The Eritreans went on the offensive, believing that the Ethiopian government would collapse. The Ethiopians quickly accepted a peace plan prepared by the Organization for African Unity (OAU), but Eritrea held back. Then in 1999, the Eritreans had a setback on the battlefield, and so realized that their huge neighbor was far better able than they to sustain a long war. They too then signed the peace plan, but the Ethiopians were no longer in the mood. The Ethiopians backed away from the plan by creating technical problems that they said prevented them from accepting a cease-fire. In May 2000, the Ethiopians launched a human wave advance at several border crossings and moved thousands of troops far into Eritrea, capturing a regional center, and bombing the airport at Eritrea's capital, Asmara. Estimates are that 120 thousand young men have died on the battlefields. Quite apart from the military casualties, the renewed fighting displaced 750 thousand Eritrean civilians who joined the some 15 million people in the horn of Africa (10.5 million were Ethiopians) facing starvation because of drought and war.

It is clear that political and economic factors and, perhaps most significant, the personal rivalry and animosity between the two leaders are more important that the original border dispute. The Prime Minister of Ethiopia, Meles Zenawi, and Eritrean President Issaias Afwerki led rebel movements in concert that defeated the Soviet-backed dictatorship of Mengistu in 1991. Eritrea, which had been an Ethiopian Province, voted to become independent and became a nation in 1993. Until about three years ago, the neighbors maintained an open border, and the level of official trust was considered to be high. However, when Eritrea became independent from Ethiopia in 1993, many issues, including their future fiscal and trade relations, were not defined. Rather they were left to the good relationship between the two leaders. The collapse of that friendship has been a disaster for both countries.

It is estimated that when the war commenced a half-million Eritreans lived in Ethiopia, and 100,000 Ethiopians lived in Eritrea. Both countries have carried out massive expulsions and issued residence permits since. This is confusing because of the extent to which Eritrean and Ethiopian heritage is shared. Intermarriage has been commonplace for generations, especially between Eritreans and natives of Tigray. In fact, the mother of Eritrea's President Issaias is Tigrayan, and his father an Eritrean. An Eritrean gave birth to Prime Minister Meles, whose father was Tigrayan. Blood, culture, and history, as well as economics and trade link the two countries. The mutual heritage of the two countries and their leaders makes this senseless war even more tragic.

It is not clear that the ceasefire agreed to in mid-2000 and monitored by the UN military peacekeeping unit will hold. Although both governments welcomed the UN, the war of words between them continued unabated. Observers note that regardless of the facts, the propaganda of both sides seems to be creating a possible pretext for resumption of the war.

Sources and Notes

[1] See Bruce Johnston and Peter Kilby, Agriculture and Structural Transformation: Economic Strategies in Late-Developing Countries, (Oxford University Press, New York, 1975).

[2] See Carl K. Eicher, *Food Security Battles in Sub-Saharan Africa,* (Monograph of a plenary address to The VII World Congress for Rural Sociology, Bologna, Italy June 26–July 2, 1988), and *Sustainable Institutions for African Agricultural Development.* Working Paper No. 19, (International Service for National Agricultural Research, The Hague, 1989).

[3] Bruce Johnston and Peter Kilby, op. cit.

[4] Food security exists when all people at all times have physical and economic access to sufficient food to meet their dietary needs for productive and healthy lives.

[5] The authority quoted is Samuel Huntington, a consultant to the Constitutional Commission established by the Transitional Government of Ethiopia. This quote is from *Ethnic Democracy: The Ethiopian Case*, a paper by Donald Crummey presented at the Annual Meetings of the African Studies Association, (Toronto, November 4, 1994), p. 11.

[6] This section draws on several media articles, including:

The Economist, "Ethiopia and Eritrea, Why are they fighting?" (*The Economist*, London, UK, June 13, 1998) p. 44.

USIA, Susan E. Rice, Assistant Secretary of State for African Affairs, "Africa at Large: Rice on U.S. Policy Options in Horn of Africa," USIA Press Release, (United States Information Agency, Washington, D.C., May 27, 1999).

The Economist, "Ethiopia's and Eritrea's forgotten war, resumed," (*The Economist*, London, UK, May 20, 2000) p. 55-56.

The Economist, "Ethiopia and Eritrea Peace? Maybe," (*The Economist*, London, UK, June 3, 2000) p. 47.

The Economist, "Eritrea, Patrolling the line," (*The Economist*, London, UK, September 30, 2000) p. 47.

Glossary

Amhara: A major ethnic group in Ethiopia, native to or descended from natives of most of the highlands of Ethiopia. Haile Selassie was an *Amhara,* however his government included many non-*Amhara* persons at all levels.

Amharic: A national language of Ethiopia spoken by the majority of its citizens.

arata: A loan.

awraja: Sub-division of a region.

birr: Ethiopian currency unit. Today about 8 *birr* = *US$1.00.* In the mid-1980s, 2075 *birr* = US$1.00.

Dejazmach: Literally "commander of the gate," a title of nobility equivalent to "Count." The highest rank was *Ras.* The second highest rank given by the Emperor to nobility or a high-level official was *Dejazmach.*

derg: An Amharic word meaning "committee or council," a common term used for the military junta that took over the government in 1974.

djanggi: An indigenous form of savings and credit in West Cameroon.

ekub: A kind of informal savings and loan association in Ethiopia.

Fitawrari: Literally "leader of the vanguard," a title of nobility equivalent to "Viscount." It was the third highest rank given by the Emperor.

gult: A fief granted by the Emperor incorporating the rights to tribute and labor from peasants on a certain piece of land.

Harambee movement: An indigenous form of savings and credit in Kenya.

idir: A kind of mutual insurance society in Ethiopia.

kebele: Sub-division of a woreda; smallest administrative area of the Ethiopian government. Similar to a U.S. township or ward.

killil: A region; the current Ethiopian government has established eight regions and two metropolitan areas (Addis Ababa and Harar).

maderia: Land granted to government employees in lieu of salary or pension.

Meskal: Feast of the True Cross, September 27th.

Ras: Literally "head," a title of nobility equivalent to "Duke." *Ras* was the highest rank given by the Emperor.

rist: A lineage system of land ownership; the hereditary right of an individual to a piece of land.

semon: The church's right to a piece of land.

teff: A cereal crop grown in the highlands of Ethiopia, the staple food of people in the highlands. Its Latin name is *eragrostice Abyssinica* or *Eragrostis teff.*

Tigrayan (also Tigrean): An ethnic group of Ethiopians native to or descended from natives of the Tigris *(also Tigre)* area in northern Ethiopia. *Tigrayan* persons dominate senior positions in the current

Ethiopian government and the private sector. It is estimated that they now control 80 percent of the national economy.

*Tigrayna (*also *Tigregna):* The language spoken by *Tigrayan* people.

woreda: a sub-district, sub-division of an awraja.

usufruct or usufruct right: The right to use of land and other real property.

Index